Anne

by Paul Ledoux

adapted from the novel

Anne of Green Gables

by L.M. Montgomery

This dramatization by playwright Paul Ledoux is
based on the novel *Anne of Green Gables*
by L. M. Montgomery and is produced with the
permission of David Macdonald, trustee
and Ruth Macdonald, who are the heirs of
L. M. Montgomery.

PLAYWRIGHTS CANADA PRESS
Toronto • Canada

Anne by Paul Ledoux © 1999 adapted from the novel
Anne of Green Gables by L.M. Montgomery.
Playwrights Canada Press: 54 Wolseley St., 2nd fl. Toronto, Ontario
CANADA M5T 1A5 Tel: (416) 703-0201 Fax: (416) 703-0059
e-mail: cdplays@interlog.com   http://www.puc.ca

Playwrights Canada Press publishes with the generous
assistance of The Canada Council for the Arts - Writing and
Publishing Section and the Ontario Arts Council.

Cover photo by Cylla von Tiedemann.

Canadian Cataloguing in Publication Data
Ledoux, Paul, 1949 —
  Anne : from the novel Anne of Green Gables by L.M. Montgomery
A play
ISBN 0-88754- 576-9
1. Shirley, Anne (Fictitious character) - Juvenile drama. 2 Children's
plays, Canadian (English)* I. Montgomery, L.M. (Lucy Maud), 1874-
1942. Anne of Green Gables. II Title.
PS8573.E3439A84 1999   jC812'.54   C99-931030-5
PR9199.3..L383A84 1999

First edition: June.,1999
Printed and bound in Winnipeg, Manitoba, Canada.

To Ferne Downey

the best of all bosom friends

Paul Ledoux was born in Halifax, Nova Scotia. He began writing for the theatre in Montreal where his play, "The Electrical Man", won the Quebec Drama Festival award for best play in 1975. He has had 28 plays produced and the majority have been musicals including: "Cheatin' Hearts" - written with David Smyth; "Hot Flashes" - written with John Roby; "Judy!" (Dora Mavor Moore Award nominee); "Honky Tonk Angels" with Ferne Downey; two collaborations with David Young: "Love Is Strange" and the Dora Mavor Moore Award and Chalmers Best Play Award-winning "Fire"; "Dream a Little Dream" a musical about The Mamas and The Papas, co-written with the group's lead singer, Denny Doherty; and "The Secret Garden", an adaptation of the novel by Francis Hobson Burnett.

INTRODUCTION BY KATE BUTLER MACDONALD

I must tell you that I was leery when my family was asked to consider the possibility of granting permission for yet another format for "Anne of Green Gables" — a dramatic stage adaptation written by Paul Ledoux for a specifically youthful audience. My grandmother's most famous novel had already been adapted for the movies, television and a musical stage play and my family and I are quite protective when it comes to "Anne Shirley" and her world.

One of the more dramatic memories of my childhood was flying on a VIP private jet with my father (Dr. Stuart Macdonald, L.M. Montgomery's younger son) to Charlottetown, PEI to unveil a plaque and be part of the launching ceremonies of the MV L. M. Montgomery — the ferry that would travel between Wood Island and the mainland. This was all arranged as part of the Centennial Year Celebrations in 1967 and we were accompanied by many prominent dignitaries and Gracie Finley who, at the time, was playing the lead role in the very successful, long-running Canadian Stage Musical play, "Anne of Green Gables". Later that year I was invited backstage to meet again with Gracie Finley and the other cast members. There is something about the magic of live theatre that can't be duplicated on screen and it was a thrilling occasion for a nine year old girl from Toronto.

The magic of the theatre has yet again thrilled me and a new generation of Montgomery's heirs. My nine-year old daughter, Eliza and ten-year old son, Graydon, and I attended the opening of Paul Ledoux's dramatic stage adaptation of "Anne" at the Young People's Theatre in Toronto in April of 1998. This is a new and fresh adaptation of Anne of Green Gables that brought back the joy of reading this novel for the first time for members of my family. Anne and her life in Avonlea came alive on stage in a charming and touching dramatic presentation evidenced by the snifflling and tears of the audience at YPT. I could feel how contemporary children could relate to this spirited girl and the endearing characters from Avonlea. I am very pleased to be introducing the reader to this theatrical adaptation of "Anne".

After you have read this adaptation, go back and enjoy the novel again!

Kate Macdonald Butler, Toronto
May, 1999

CHARACTERS

The play takes place over a period of about five years, with the children growing up in the process. Their ages are indicated accordingly.

MARILLA CUTHBERT a tall, thin angular woman; dark hair with some gray streaks twisted up in a hard little knot behind. A woman of narrow experience and rigid conscience, with something about her mouth which might be indicative of a sense of humour.

MATTHEW CUTHBERT Marilla's brother. A painfully shy farmer in his sixties, but with a stubborn streak and a warm heart. He is described in *Anne of Green Gables* as an ungainly figure with long iron-gray hair that touches his stooping shoulders, and a full, soft brown beard.

ANNE SHIRLEY A vivacious orphan child - 13 to 17. She much freckled with bright red hair, her eyes full of spirit and vivacity; mercurial, overly dramatic, intelligent, in need of love.

DIANA BARRY Anne's best friend - 13 to 17. A very pretty little girl, with black eyes and hair, and rosy cheeks, and a merry expression. Not as clever as Anne, but she has a big heart and real charm. Diana often laughs before she speaks.

RACHEL LYNDE The town's busiest and nosiest leader. Mid-forties. A fat woman who waddles. One of those delightful and popular people who pride themselves on speaking their mind without fear or favour.

GILBERT BLYTHE

Anne's chief competitor and love interest - 14 to 18. A tall boy, with curly brown hair, roguish hazel eyes, and a mouth twisted into a teasing smile. Gilbert is older that the girls because he had to leave school for a year. He is very intelligent and ambitious.

RUBY GILLIS

A friend of Anne - 13 to 17. Ruby is romantic, pretty and, in terms of her interest in other peoples business, a 'kindred spirit' of Rachel's. Large, bright-blue eyes, a brilliant complexion, and a plump showy figure. She laughs a great deal, is cheerful and good-tempered, and enjoys the pleasant things of life.

JOSIE PYE

Anne's most troublesome friend - 13 to 17. "Josie is a Pye, so she can't help being disagreeable." Josie Pye is jealous, catty, clever, mischievous and an all-round excellent foil for Anne.

THE SET

The action in "Anne" must move fluidly from location to location and through a number of time periods including Anne's return to Avonlea after Queens and her years growing up in Avonlea. The action must move quickly between playing areas that include the interior at Green Gables; kitchen, parlor and upstairs room for Anne.; the train station, the road to Avonlea, Rachel Lynde's front porch and the interior of the Gillis store and Barry house.

MUSIC

While not a traditional musical in any sense of the word, Anne uses children's rhyming songs and snippets of folk songs and poems to help create the world of Avonlea. In addition, the play uses "The Island Hymn" an original lyric by L.M. Montgomery which was set to "God Save The Queen". Songs are sung without accompaniment or, when called for, with on-stage piano.

"Anne" premiered at The Young People's Theatre, Toronto, on April 5, 1998, with the following cast:

MARILLA CUTHBURT   *Janet Amos*
RACHEL LYNDE   *Robin Craig*
MATTHEW CUTHBURT   *Jerry Franken*
DIANA BARRY   *Catherine Gatotos*
JOSIE PYE   *Carolyn Hay*
ANNE SHIRLEY   *Jennie Raymond*
GILBERT BLYTHE   *Jamie Robinson*
RUBY GILLIS   *Eliza-Jane Scott*

Directed by Patricia Vanstone.
Adaptation by Paul Ledoux.
Music by Ian Tamblyn.
Lights by Steven Hawkins.
Set and Costumes by Sue LePage.
Stage Manager - Nancy Dryden.
Assistant Stage Manager - Michael Sinclair.

Act One, Scene One

The Train Station. Avonlea.
RUBY and RACHEL enter and stand in
animated but unheard conversation, then
break apart as JOSIE and DIANA enter.

RUBY   Josie!

RACHEL   Diana! Have you heard the news?

RUBY   Anne...

RACHEL   Anne Shirley...

RUBY &
RACHEL   ...has won the Avery Scholarship!

              MATTHEW and MARILLA enter, unnoticed.

DIANA   The Avery!

JOSIE   That's impossible! A girl has never won the
              Avery Scholarship and I won't believe Anne
              Shirley is the first.

MARILLA   Believe what you will, Josie Pye, it won't alter
              the fact that our Anne has won full tuition to
              Richmond University.

MATTHEW   In Halifax!

RUBY   *(sighs)* In Halifax.

              DIANA and JOSIE go rushing up to
              MATTHEW. He tries to elude their
              enthusiastic attention.

JOSIE   When did you find out, Mr. Cuthbert?

MATTHEW   Well now.... ah....

RACHEL   It was in the Charlottetown paper.

DIANA   But, we get the Charlottetown paper every night and...

MATTHEW   No, not last night... it was in... ah...

MARILLA   It was in this morning's paper — the eye doctor brought it out with him.

RUBY   The eye doctor?

RACHEL   He came out from Charlottetown this morning — to examine Marilla.

DIANA   You're having trouble with your eyes?

A flurry of concern from the women.

MARILLA   It's nothing anyone should concern themselves with.

DIANA   But Marilla....

MARILLA   It's nothing! Just some new glasses. In any case, the doctor had the morning paper and right on the front page — there it was.

JOSIE   The front page. Oh, Mr. Cuthbert!

Sound of the train pulling in.

MATTHEW   Yup, yup, front page.

RACHEL   "Avonlea Girl Wins Avery."

MATTHEW   Here she comes! I mean, Anne... she's... oh...

MATTHEW rushes off. The girls laugh.

JOSIE   Marilla, your brother is still absolutely the shyest man in the whole world.

MARILLA   It's his chief virtue if you ask me. And he's right excited. Anne's on the train.

           MARILLA walks upstage looking towards the platform. RACHEL follows.

JOSIE   Well, I couldn't be more shocked. I mean, everyone expected Gilbert Blythe to win that scholarship. Gilbert was first in the class at Queen's, you know.

RUBY   But Anne could always beat Gilbert in English and The Avery is for English.

MARILLA   *(sees ANNE)* Anne!

           A squeal and a cheer from the girls. ANNE walks on with MATTHEW. They rush to greet her as she works her way towards MARILLA.

RUBY   Congratulations, Anne!

ANNE   Thank you, Ruby.

JOSIE   Yes, congratulations.

ANNE   Josie.

DIANA   Oh Anne, Halifax!

ANNE   Yes, Diana. Halifax.

RACHEL   A girl from Avonlea in university, the whole town will be abuzz.

MARILLA   We're all so proud of you, Anne.

ANNE   *(taking her hand and squeezing it)* Thank you, Marilla. I missed you and Matthew, so much.

MATTHEW   *(to ANNE)* Well now, we thought maybe what with the teacher's college and all, you just might forget about Marilla Cuthbert and her old brother.

ANNE   Oh Matthew, I thought about you both every
                night and I was so lonesome for dear old Green
                Gables.

MATTHEW   Well, you're home now... and... and... Hail the
                conquering Scholar!

                *Everyone laughs and applauds. MATTHEW is
                embarrassed.*

MATTHEW   Ah... ah... best get the trunk. *(exiting past
                GILBERT who enters, carrying his case)* Gilbert.

JOSIE   Gilbert, you're not due back until tomorrow.

GILBERT   No, but...no reason to stay in town.

JOSIE   Congratulations on coming first. I knew you
                would.

GILBERT   Thank you, Josie. *(to RACHEL)* Mrs. Lynde, my
                father wrote that there is a possibility of a
                teaching position here in Avonlea. I'll be
                applying.

RACHEL   You can count on my support, Mr. Blythe.

JOSIE   Did you hear that, everyone? Gilbert is going
                to stay in Avonlea and teach!

ANNE   You're not going to Richmond?

JOSIE   'lantic Ocean! Can I believe my ears? Anne
                Shirley just spoke to Gilbert Blythe.

GILBERT   No, not this year, Anne. I have to earn some
                tuition money first.

JOSIE   *(to ANNE)* It will be hard for you to excel
                without Gilbert to beat, won't it?

GILBERT
& ANNE   Honestly, Josie.

JOSIE	It's the simple truth and everybody knows it.
GILBERT	Ah... well, I didn't get a chance to say it before now, but congratulations on your win, Anne.

He offers ANNE his hand. They shake.

You deserve it.

ANNE	Gilbert.
GILBERT	Good day.

GILBERT exits.

JOSIE	*(chasing GILBERT off)* Gilbert wait, I have the surrey if you need a ride home!

MATTHEW re-enters.

MATTHEW	Trunk's on the wagon. Let's go home.
ANNE	Yes, let's go home. Will you come over after supper, Diana?
DIANA	Put a candle in the window and I will fly to your side.
ANNE	And Ruby, you'll come for tea tomorrow morning?
RUBY	I'd love to.

MATTHEW, ANNE and MARILLA exit.

DIANA	Well, I should be off too. Do come tomorrow, Ruby. I still haven't heard anything at all of your adventures at Queen's.
RUBY	Well, I didn't win a scholarship, but I was crowned handsomest girl of the year. And, I shouldn't gossip, but Josie gained eminence as the sharpest-tongued young lady at Queen's.

DIANA	She did!
RUBY	That's right, and she never stopped chasing Gilbert Blythe, not for one second!
DIANA	Poor Josie, she still can't resist Gilbert Blythe.
RUBY	No one ever could.
DIANA	Except Anne. (*as she exits*) See you tomorrow — at eleven!
RUBY	Bye, Diana. Do you remember the day Anne arrived in Avonlea, Mrs. Lynde?
RACHEL	Clearly. It fair drove me to distraction seeing Matthew drive by that afternoon. Now, as you know Ruby, I always keep a sharp eye on everything that passes by.
RUBY	It is 'your duty as your house sits so convenient on the crossroads.'
RACHEL	That's right and if I notice anything odd or out of place. Well! You can just imagine how I felt when I saw Matthew Cuthbert ride by in his buggy, at half-past three on the afternoon during planting season, in his best suit of clothes...
RUBY	It must have driven you to distraction.
RACHEL	I could make nothing of it. Nothing.
RUBY	Matthew Cuthbert would never go to town at that time of year.
RACHEL	Never! So, I set out for Green Gables right away to find out what was what.
RUBY	I was at the station that day, as you'll recall.
RACHEL	That's right, you were on the same train that brought Anne to Avonlea.

RUBY   I was coming back from Charlottetown and...
        well , she was the queerest looking girl you
        ever saw and I swear she didn't stop talking,
        not for a moment, from the time I got on the
        train until the moment I got off. 'Course I
        heard Mrs. Spencer say she was for the
        Cuthberts, so, when I saw Mr. Cuthbert drive
        up I wasn't the least surprised.

Act One, Scene Two

The Train Station. Avonlea. Four Years Earlier.
DIANA and JOSIE come on playing hide
and seek. GILBERT runs through and teases
them, then runs off as MATTHEW walks on.

JOSIE   Hello, Sir!

MATTHEW starts, looks uncomfortable and
nods. He turns away.

JOSIE   Lovely evening, isn't it?

MATTHEW   *(almost jumps)* Well now. I... I... lovely.

DIANA and JOSIE run off. MATTHEW
walks towards the station. On the platform we
find ANNE sitting on a bench. This is the
young ANNE, dressed in a tattered orphan's
dress. She looks tense — rigidity and
expectation in her attitude and expression.
MATTHEW tries to sidle past ANNE as
quickly as possible without looking at her. She
stares at him. He glances at her, glances away
and glances back again. Suddenly she bounds
to her feet. He jumps.

ANNE   I suppose you are Mr. Matthew Cuthbert of
Green Gables? I am very glad you've come. I
was beginning to be afraid you weren't coming
for me and I was imagining all the horrible
things that could have happened to prevent
you. I had made up my mind that if you didn't
come, I'd go down the track to that big wild
cherry-tree at the bend, and climb up into it to
stay all night. It would be lovely to sleep in a
wild cherry-tree all white with bloom in the

moonshine, don't you think? I wouldn't be a bit afraid.

MATTHEW   Ah... Well now, the horse is over in the yard. Give me your bag.

ANNE   Oh, I can carry it. I've got all my worldly goods in it, but it isn't heavy. And if it isn't carried in just a certain way the handle pulls out — so I'd better keep it because I know the exact knack of it.

> *As she picks up the bag, the handle breaks. She carries the bag off in her arms.*

Oh, I'm very glad you've come, even if it would have been nice to sleep in a cherry-tree.

MATTHEW   *(watching her go)* Well now.

> *MATTHEW follows ANNE off.*

Act One, Scene Three

Green Gables.
The back porch. RACHEL approaches.

RACHEL   It's no wonder Matthew and Marilla are both a little odd, living way back off the road by themselves. I'd not call living in such a place living at all. It's just staying, that's what. *(calling off)* Marilla!

MARILLA comes to the door.

MARILLA   Rachel, what took you so long?

RACHEL   Marilla, I saw Matthew driving to town and— Took me so long?

MARILLA   Come in, I'm making tea.

MARILLA leads RACHEL inside the darkened kitchen.

RACHEL   I... I thought maybe you were having one of your bad headaches and he was gone for the Doctor.

MARILLA   There's no call for a doctor.

RACHEL   Then what is going on?

MARILLA   It's nothing really, Rachel.

RACHEL   Marilla, three places are laid. That is more than nothing!

MARILLA   Oh, for goodness sake, Rachel, it's of no importance. Matthew is getting up in years, you know, and he isn't as spry as he once was.

So, when we heard Mrs. Spencer was going over to get a little girl from the orphanage in Halifax, we sent her word to bring us a smart, likely boy to help out around the place.

RACHEL   An orphan boy!

MARILLA   He's coming on the train tonight.

RACHEL   Marilla, bringing a strange child into your house and home? Why, only last week I read in the paper how a man and his wife up west of the Island took a boy out of an orphan asylum and he set fire to the house — set it on purpose, Marilla — and burnt them to a crisp.

MARILLA   To a crisp?

RACHEL   To a crisp, and I know another case where an adopted boy used to suck the eggs.

MARILLA   Suck the eggs!

RACHEL   They couldn't break him of it. If you had asked my advice in the matter, which you didn't do, Marilla, I'd have said; "For mercy's sake don't even think of such a thing."

MARILLA   *(sighs)* Oh, I don't deny there's something in what you say, Rachel, but Matthew has set his mind to it and it's so seldom Matthew sets his mind on anything, that I feel it's my duty to give in.

RACHEL   Yes, well, it couldn't have happened at a worse time. I'll be off to Carmody tomorrow and not back until my eldest, Mary, has delivered her third child, so I'll be of no help in dealing with the orphan.

MARILLA   Well, it will be a great hardship for us, I'm sure, but I suppose we'll just have to struggle along and hope for the best.

RACHEL   I suppose you will. I just pray he doesn't put
            poison in the well. An orphan over in New
            Brunswick did that and the whole family died
            in fearful agonies. Only, it was a girl in that
            instance.

MARILLA   Well, we're not getting a girl. I'd never dream
            of taking a girl, so that is of no concern.

Act One, Scene Four

The Avenue.
MATTHEW and ANNE drive through a
cherry orchard at dusk. The children create an
archway of cherry blossoms for them to drive
through.

On tape we hear the children singing a
nursery rhyme — In And Out The Window.

CHILDREN   *(tape)* Go in and out the window.
Go in and out the window.
To see what we can see
Go round and round the village
Go round and round the village
To see what we can see

ANNE   What is this place called?

MATTHEW   The Avenue.

ANNE   Oh no, it's too beautiful for that. We have to
think of a better name, Matthew. I know! We
can call it The White Way of Delight. That
would be a fitting name because there are
cherry-trees in bloom everywhere, aren't there!

MATTHEW   Ah... yup.

ANNE   This is the bloomiest place in the whole
world! Even more beautiful than I'd imagined.
It's delightful when your imaginings come true,
isn't it.

MATTHEW   Well now, I don't know.

ANNE   Am I talking too much? People are always telling me I do. If you say so, I'll stop. I can stop when I make up my mind to it, although it's difficult.

MATTHEW   Oh, you can talk as much as you like. I don't mind.

ANNE   Oh, I'm so glad. It's such a relief to talk when one wants to and not be told that children should be seen and not heard. *(beat)* I feel pretty nearly perfectly happy. I can't feel exactly perfectly happy because — well, what colour would you call this?

               She twitches one of her long glossy braids over her thin shoulder.

MATTHEW   It's red, ain't it?

ANNE   *(a sigh that seems to come from her very toes)* Yes, it's red. Now you see why I can't be perfectly happy. I don't mind the other things so much — the freckles and the green eyes and my skinniness. I can imagine them away. But I cannot imagine red hair away. It will be my lifelong sorrow that I am so homely. Which would you rather be if you had the choice — divinely beautiful or dazzlingly clever or angelically good?

MATTHEW   Well now, I— I don't know exactly.

ANNE   Neither do I. I can never decide. But it doesn't make much real difference for it isn't likely I'll ever be either. It's certain I'll never be angelically good. *(pause)* Oh, isn't that pretty!

MATTHEW   That's Barry's Pond.

ANNE   The water's the most spiritual shadings of crocus and rose and ethereal green, with elusive tints for which no name has ever been found! I shall call it — let me see — the Lake of Shining Waters. Isn't that a nice imaginative name?

MATTHEW   Well now...

ANNE   I am convinced that is the right name for it. I know because of the thrill. When I hit on a name that suits exactly, it gives me a thrill. Do things ever give you a thrill?

MATTHEW   Well now, yes. It always kind of gives me a thrill to see them ugly white grubs that spade up in the cucumber beds. I hate the look of them.

ANNE   Oh, I don't think that can be exactly the same kind of a thrill. There doesn't seem to be much connection between grubs and lakes of shining waters, does there?

MATTHEW   Well... That's Green Gables over—

ANNE   Oh, don't tell me — let me guess. I'm sure I'll guess right. (*ANNE closes her eyes and then opens them and looks around.*) There... the house away to the left, far back from the road. The one surrounded by the blossoming apple trees with the crystal-white star over it... shining like a lamp of guidance and promise. That is my new home!

            Transition. The children run on playing hide and seek.

JOSIE   (*tape*) Diana, I can hear your mother calling you.

DIANA   (*tape*) Coming! Bye!

GILBERT   (*tape*) Cows need milkin'.

RUBY   (*tape*) See you tomorrow.

JOSIE   (*tape*) Gilbert, wait up!

Act One, Scene Five

Green Gables.
ANNE and MATTHEW enter. MARILLA is
sitting on the back porch peeling potatoes.

ANNE   *(to MATTHEW)* It seems so wonderful that I'm going to live with you and belong to you. I've never belonged to anybody — not really.

MARILLA   Matthew Cuthbert, where is the boy?

MATTHEW   *(wretchedly)* There wasn't any boy. There was only her.

MARILLA   Well, this is a pretty piece of business!

ANNE drops her bag and clasps her hands.

ANNE   You don't want me! You don't want me because I'm not a boy! *(bursts into tears)* I might have known it was all too beautiful to last. Nobody ever did want me.

MARILLA   Now, now, there's no need to cry, child... What's her name?

MATTHEW   Well, now...I forgot to ask.

ANNE   *(eagerly)* Will you please call me Cordelia?

MARILLA   Call you Cordelia? Is that your name?

ANNE   No-o-o, it's not exactly my name, but I would love to be called Cordelia. It's such a perfectly elegant name.

MARILLA   I don't know what on earth you mean. If Cordelia isn't your name, what is?

ANNE   Anne Shirley, but, oh, please do call me
            Cordelia. It can't matter much to you what you
            call me if I'm only going to be here a little
            while, can it? And Anne is such an unromantic
            name.

MARILLA   Unromantic, fiddlesticks! Anne is a real good,
            plain, sensible name.

ANNE   If you call me Anne, please call me Anne
            spelled with an E?

MARILLA   *(a rusty smile flickers)* What difference does it
            make how it's spelled?

ANNE   Oh, it makes such a difference. When you hear
            a name pronounced, can't you always see it in
            your mind, just as if it was printed out? I can
            and A-n-n looks dreadful, but A-n-n-e looks so
            much more distinguished. If you'll only call me
            Anne spelled with an E, I shall try to reconcile
            myself to not being called Cordelia.

MARILLA   Very well, then, Anne spelled with an E, can
            you tell us how this mistake came to be made?

ANNE   I don't know. Mrs. Spencer said distinctly that
            you wanted a girl. *(reproachfully, turning to
            MATTHEW)* Oh, why didn't you tell me at the
            station that you didn't want me and leave me
            there?

MATTHEW   Well now, I just couldn't think how to say it.

MARILLA   I'm sorry, child. We wanted a boy to help
            Matthew on the farm. A girl is of no use to us.

ANNE   *(sighs)* I am in the depths of despair. Have you
            ever been in the depths of despair?

MARILLA   No, I've never been in the depths of despair.

ANNE   Well, did you ever try to imagine you were in
            the depths of despair?

MARILLA   No, I didn't. Go put your bag in the spare room, top of the stairs.

ANNE   It's a very uncomfortable feeling indeed.

MARILLA   Oh! Shoo!

> *MARILLA points imperiously and ANNE goes upstairs.*

MARILLA   Well, this is a pretty kettle of fish. She'll have to be sent back to the asylum.

MATTHEW   It's kind of a pity to send her back when she's so set on staying here.

MARILLA   But what good would she be to us?

MATTHEW   We might be some good to her.

MARILLA   Matthew Cuthbert, I believe that child has bewitched you!

MATTHEW   She's a real interesting little thing, Marilla. You should have heard her talk coming from the station.

MARILLA   Oh, she can talk fast enough. I saw that at once. It's nothing in her favour, either. She's got to be dispatched straight-way back to where she came from.

MATTHEW   Well now, it's just as you say, of course. We can talk it over again tomorrow.

> *Music bridges to early morning and next scene.*

Act One, Scene Six

Green Gables.
ANNE looks out her bedroom window.

ANNE   This is as lovely as anything I've ever dreamed. Oh, there is scope for imagination here!

MARILLA enters. She's wearing her best dress and her mother's amethyst brooch.

ANNE   Isn't it wonderful?

MARILLA   What?

ANNE   Everything! That big old cherry tree for instance - so thick-set with blossoms that hardly a leaf is to be seen.

MARILLA   It's a big tree and it blooms great, but the fruit don't amount to much never — small and wormy.

ANNE   Still, it blooms as if it meant it.

MARILLA looks at the tangle of ANNE's hair and begins to try and fix it up.

ANNE   I've been imagining that it was really me you wanted after all and that I was to stay here for ever and ever. And every spring Matthew and I would climb high into the cherry tree and—

MARILLA   For pity's sake, hold your tongue. You talk entirely too much for a little girl.

ANNE   Sorry.

MARILLA   What's to be done with you, I don't know.
          Matthew is a most ridiculous man.

ANNE   I think he's lovely. I felt that he was a
          kindred spirit as soon as I saw him.

MARILLA   You're both queer enough, if that's what you
          mean by kindred spirits.

          A pause. MARILLA struggles with the hair.
          ANNE looks up at her.

ANNE   What is the stone in that brooch you are
          wearing, Miss Cuthbert?

MARILLA   It is amethyst.

ANNE   It's so beautiful, it makes you look like a... a
          Queen.

MARILLA   It was my mother's. She was just a plain
          farmer's wife and that was good enough for
          her.

ANNE   I think to be a farmer's wife in Avonlea is as
          good as being a Queen.

MARILLA   Shuss.

ANNE   Sorry.

          MARILLA continues to awkwardly fix her
          hair.

ANNE   Did you ever know of anybody whose hair was
          red when she was young, but got to be another
          colour when she grew up?

MARILLA   No, and I shouldn't think it likely to happen
          in your case either.

ANNE   *(sighs)* Well, that is another hope gone. 'My
          life is a perfect graveyard of buried hopes.'
          That's a sentence I read in a book once, and I

say it over to comfort myself whenever I'm disappointed in anything.

MARILLA   As you're evidently bent on talking you might as well talk to some purpose by telling me what you know about yourself. (*as ANNE takes a deep breath, MARILLA jumps back in*) And just stick to bald facts.

ANNE   I was born in Nova Scotia and turned thirteen last March. My mother's name was Bertha Shirley and my father's name was Walter Shirley. They were teachers. I believe a good teacher is worth their weight in gold, don't you?.

MARILLA   It's a job that needs doing, that's for certain. What happened to your parents?

ANNE   They died of fever when I was just three months old. That left me an orphan. Mrs. Thomas said folks were at their wits' end. Nobody wanted me even then. It seems to be my fate.

MARILLA   Who was Mrs. Thomas?

ANNE   A woman who worked for my mother cleaning. I had no relatives so Mrs. Thomas said she'd take me, though she was poor and had a drunken husband. When I got big enough I helped look after the Thomas children There were four of them and I can tell you they took a lot of looking after.

MARILLA   Why did she send you to the orphanage?

ANNE   Oh, she didn't! Mr. Thomas was killed falling under a train. His mother offered to take Mrs. Thomas and the children, but she didn't want me. So, Mrs. Hammond said she'd take me as I was handy with children.

Mrs. Hammond had twins three times. I like babies in moderation, but twins three times in succession is too much. I told Mrs. Hammond so firmly, after the last pair. I used to get so dreadfully tired carrying them about.

MARILLA   Yes, I suppose you would.

ANNE   I lived with the Hammonds until Mrs. Hammond died and then I had to go to the asylum in Halifax.

MARILLA   Were those women — Mrs. Thomas and Mrs. Hammond — good to you?

ANNE   O-o-o-h... Oh, they meant to be — I know they meant to be just as good and kind as possible. But it's very trying to have a drunken husband and it must be even more trying to have twins three times in succession, don't you think?

             MATTHEW enters below and yells up the stairs.

MATTHEW   I took your message to Mrs. Spencer.

             MARILLA comes down, followed by ANNE.

MARILLA   Did she explain what happened?

MATTHEW   She said it was our own fault for sending word by her brother, who's stupid as a post. And I said you were of a mind to send Anne back and then...

             He pulls out a small paper bag and hands it to ANNE.

MATTHEW   Ah... I heard you young ones liked chocolate sweeties, so I got you some.

             ANNE takes the candies and is about to eat one. MARILLA glares at MATTHEW.

MARILLA   It'll ruin her teeth and stomach.

> *ANNE stops, candy just about in her mouth.*

There, there child don't look so dismal. You can eat those since Matthew has gone and got them, just don't sicken yourself eating them all at once.

> *ANNE pops candy into her mouth,*

(*to MATTHEW*) Well, what did Mrs. Spencer say?

MATTHEW   She couldn't get a word in edgeways. That Hester Blewett was there!

MARILLA   Hester Blewett!

ANNE   Who is Hester Blewett?

MATTHEW   The most stingy, quarrelsome woman in all of White Sands is who. And everybody knows it.

ANNE   Oh. Somehow this feels like the end of everything.

MATTHEW   She said that as she was due soon, she thought she might have use for a hard-working girl so long as she didn't eat too much.

ANNE   Due soon?

MARILLA   With her eighth baby.

ANNE   Oh.

> *ANNE glumly puts another candy in her mouth.*

MARILLA   Anne, take your candy outside and go play. Matthew and I must have a talk.

> *ANNE slumps out of the house. Then, overwhelmed by the country-side, she rushes off*

MATTHEW   I wouldn't give a dog I liked to that Blewett woman.

MARILLA   Oh Matthew, the mute misery on her face, like a creature caught in a trap she thought she had escaped. If I deny the appeal of that look, it will haunt me to my dying day.

MATTHEW   Are you saying she can stay?

> *ANNE re-enters and seeing a flower, climbs the garden trellis to pick it. She's in a precarious position by the time MARILLA goes to call her.*

MARILLA   Yes, Matthew, she may stay. But you're not to interfere. Perhaps an old maid doesn't know much about bringing up a child, but I guess she knows more than an old bachelor. When I fail, it'll be time enough to put your oar in.

MATTHEW   You can have your own way.

MARILLA   I will. *(looking out the door and terrified ANNE may fall)* Anne! Get down from there and come in! *(to MATTHEW)* I've never brought up a child, especially a girl, and I dare say I'll make a terrible mess of it. But I'll do my best.

> *ANNE rushes back in.*

ANNE   I'm sorry I climbed the trellis, Miss Cuthbert, but I saw some children playing in the woods and I thought—

MARILLA   It doesn't matter, child.

ANNE   It's final then, I am to go to Hester Blewett.

MARILLA   Well, she certainly needs you more than we do but... Matthew and I have decided to keep you.

ANNE begins to cry.

ANNE You will? You will keep me? Oh, I'm glad as glad can be. Oh, it's something more than glad. I'm so happy.

MARILLA Why, child, whatever is the matter? You're crying.

ANNE I know. I can't think why.

MARILLA Try to calm yourself. I'm afraid you both cry and laugh far too easily. And mind, if you're not good we may yet conclude to let Mrs. Blewett take you.

ANNE I'll try to be so good. It will be uphill work, I expect. What am I to call you? Shall I always say, Miss Cuthbert?

MARILLA No, you'll call me just plain Marilla. I'm not used to being called Miss Cuthbert and it would make me nervous.

ANNE It sounds awfully disrespectful to just say Marilla.

MARILLA I guess there'll be nothing disrespectful in it if you're careful to speak respectfully.

ANNE Can I call you Aunt Marilla? I'd love to call you Aunt Marilla. I've never had an aunt or any relation at all — not even a grandmother. It would make me feel as if I really belonged to you — Aunt Marilla.

MARILLA I'm not your aunt and I don't believe in calling people names that don't belong to them.

ANNE But we could imagine you were my aunt.

MARILLA I couldn't.

ANNE   Don't you ever imagine things different from
            what they really are?

MARILLA   No.

ANNE   Oh! Oh, Marilla, how much you miss!

MARILLA   *(holds her head)* Oh child, go back outside and
            play.

ANNE   May I? There is so much to see and discover
            and learn to love here that I am sure it will
            keep me busy forever!

MARILLA   Go on child, have a look around, but be home
            in time for dinner. It's served at twelve sharp.
            Twelve sharp, mind — we are very punctual
            here at Green Gables.

ANNE   Oh, thank you, Marilla, thank you, Matthew.
            From the very depths of my soul — thank you!

            *ANNE squeezes her hand and kisses
            MATTHEW, then runs off.*

MATTHEW   Ain't she something interesting?

Act One, Scene Seven

The Store.
RACHEL is giving RUBY, who is working in
her father's store, some letters to mail. RUBY
hands her a box.

RACHEL   And is there anything in the mails for The
           Lyndes?

RUBY   Not today, Mrs. Lynde. But Josie Pye was by.
           She says Gilbert has made formal application
           to the school.

RACHEL   Yes he has, and, if I know anything at all
           about the Board of Trustees, the job is his. Did
           you notice how both Gilbert and Anne jumped
           at Josie at the station?

RUBY   "Honestly Josie!" *(laughs)* I suppose that is the
           first time they were ever in agreement over
           anything since the first day Anne arrived in
           Avonlea. Do you remember when the Cuthberts
           decided to keep her?

RACHEL   No, by the time I got back summer was upon us. I
           felt like half a decade had slipped by rather
           than a month! So, just as soon as I was unpacked,
           well — you can imagine. I mean, I'd been away
           so long that Marilla, poor thing, had made three
           dresses for the girl all on her own!

           Musical bridge. The young DIANA, GILBERT
           and JOSIE play as they sing Jenny Jenkins.

CHILDREN   Oh will you wear red oh my dear, oh my dear
           Oh will you wear red Jenny Jenkins?
           No I won't wear red it's the colour of my head
           But I'll buy me a folly, rolly, tilly tolly

Cause a double roll & roll away to find me
Roll Jennie Jenkins roll

Act One, Scene Eight

Green Gables.
The younger ANNE is standing in the kitchen
wearing a very plain dress. Two more are laid
out on the table. MARILLA solemnly looks at
her handiwork. All the dresses are made alike
— plain skirts fitted tightly to plain waists,
with tight sleeves.

MARILLA   How do you like them?

ANNE   I'll imagine that I like them.

MARILLA   Imagine it! What is the matter with them?

ANNE   *(reluctantly)* They're--they're not--pretty.

MARILLA   Pretty! I don't believe in pampering vanity,
Anne, I'll tell you that right off.

ANNE   But having pretty things isn't always just
vanity, Marilla. You have your amethyst
brooch and you aren't vain.

MARILLA   These are good, sensible dresses, without any
frills or furbelows about them. I should think
you'd be grateful to get most anything.

ANNE   Oh, I am grateful, but if... if you'd make just
one with puffed sleeves it would give me such
a thrill, Marilla! Puffed sleeves are so
fashionable now.

MARILLA   Well, you'll have to do without your thrill.
Puffed sleeves are ridiculous-looking things and
a waste of good material.

ANNE   (*mournfully*) But I'd rather look ridiculous along with everybody else, than plain all by myself.

MARILLA   Go and hang up those dresses carefully in the closet.

ANNE   Yes, Marilla. (*exiting*) I'll just imagine that this one is of snow-white muslin with lovely lace frills and three-puffed sleeves.

> *ANNE walks off with her dresses. A beat and then RACHEL comes hurrying on.*

RACHEL   Marilla! Marilla!

MARILLA   I'm here Rachel, no need to hurt yourself yelling.

RACHEL   I've come to meet your orphan. What a surprise. Couldn't you have sent her back?

MARILLA   I suppose we could, but... Matthew took a fancy to her. And I must say she's a real bright little thing. The house seems a different place already. Anne! Come downstairs.

RACHEL   It's a great responsibility, no doubt about that. There's no guessing how a child like that will turn out. But I don't want to discourage you, Marilla.

MARILLA   I'm not in the least discouraged, Rachel. When I make up my mind to do something it stays made up.

> *ANNE comes running in wearing the prettiest of the dresses.*

MARILLA   Anne, this is our neighbour Mrs. Lynde.

RACHEL   Oh, Marilla, she's so terrible homely and skinny! They didn't pick you for your looks, that's sure and certain girl. Lawful heart, did any one ever see such freckles? And hair as red as carrots!

> *ANNE, face scarlet with anger and her whole slender form trembling, advances on RACHEL.*

ANNE   Carrots! How dare you! You are a rude, impolite, unfeeling woman! I hate you, I hate you, I hate you!

MARILLA   Anne!

ANNE   How would you like me to say such things about you?

RACHEL   Why...Why... Why...

ANNE   You are fat and clumsy and probably haven't a spark of imagination in you!

RACHEL   Did anybody ever see such a temper!

ANNE   Temper!

MARILLA   Anne, go to your room!

ANNE   You have hurt me worse than I have ever been hurt before and I'll never forgive you.

> *ANNE, bursts into tears, rushes to her room.*

ANNE   Never, never, never!

RACHEL   Well, there is no telling what an orphan girl can do. I don't envy you your job bringing that up, Marilla.

MARILLA   You shouldn't have twitted her about her looks, Rachel.

RACHEL   Marilla Cuthbert, you don't mean to say that you are upholding her in such a terrible display of temper?

MARILLA   No, but she's never been taught what is right. And you were too hard on her, Rachel.

RACHEL   Well, I see that I'll have to be very careful what I say after this, Marilla, since the fine feelings of orphans have to be considered before anything else. Good day, Marilla. I hope you'll come down to see me as you can't expect me to visit here again.

               RACHEL exits and MARILLA goes up to ANNE's room where ANNE sits looking miserable.

MARILLA   Anne! How could you display such temper before Mrs. Rachel Lynde, of all people! Aren't you ashamed of yourself?

ANNE   She hadn't any right to call me ugly and redheaded.

MARILLA   You say it yourself often enough.

ANNE   There's a difference between saying a thing yourself and hearing other people say it. Something just rose right up in me and I had to fly out at her.

               MATTHEW enters and calls up the stairs.

MATTHEW   Marilla? Rachel... she just, well... she... she just give me an earful!

MARILLA   I'm not surprised! Anne made a fine exhibition of herself and Mrs. Lynde will have a nice story to tell everywhere! *(to ANNE)* And she'll tell it, too!

ANNE   I'm sorry, Marilla, I'm sorry I've vexed you; but I'm glad I told her just what I did. It was a great satisfaction.

MARILLA	*(softer)* Rachel is too outspoken, but that is no excuse. She was an elder and my visitor. You should have been respectful, but you were rude and saucy and now — you must go and ask her to forgive you.
ANNE	You can punish me in any way you like, Marilla. You can shut me up in a dark, damp dungeon inhabited by snakes and toads and feed me only on bread and water and I shall not complain. But I cannot ask Mrs. Lynde to forgive me.
MARILLA	I'm not in the habit of shutting people up in dark damp dungeons They're rather scarce in Avonlea. But apologize to Mrs. Lynde you must. *(exiting)* And you'll stay in your room until you tell me you're willing to do it.
ANNE	*(mournfully)* I shall have to stay there forever then, because I can't say I'm sorry when I'm not and I can't even imagine I'm sorry.

MARILLA comes down the stairs to MATTHEW.

MATTHEW	It's a good thing Rachel Lynde got a calling down. She's a meddlesome old gossip.
MARILLA	Matthew Cuthbert, I'm astonished at you. Anne's behavior was dreadful! I suppose you'll be saying next thing that she oughtn't to be punished at all!
MATTHEW	Well now — no — not exactly. I reckon she ought to be punished... a little... But—
MARILLA	She'll stay in her room until she's willing to apologize to Mrs. Lynde, and that's final, Matthew. Now, I am going to feed the chickens.

> MARILLA exits. MATTHEW watches her go
> and then quickly goes to the stairs and calls to
> ANNE. A whispered conversation.

MATTHEW   Anne can you hear me?

ANNE   Yes, Matthew I can hear you.

MATTHEW   Then come on down here for a minute.

ANNE   I can't.

MATTHEW   Marilla's out now and I need to talk to you.

ANNE   Very well, Matthew. I'll risk her wrath again... for you.

> ANNE enters.

MATTHEW   Anne, don't you think you'd better do it and have it over with? It'll have to be done sooner or later, you know, for Marilla's a dreadful determined woman — dreadful determined.

ANNE   Do you mean apologize to Mrs. Lynde?

MATTHEW   (*eagerly*) Just smooth it over so to speak. That's what I was trying to get at.

ANNE   Oh, Matthew. It would be true enough to say I am sorry, because I am sorry now. I was mad clear through but now I feel so ashamed of myself. It would be humiliating. But, I'd do anything for you — if you really want me to.

MATTHEW   Well now, of course I do. It'd be terrible lonesome downstairs without you. Just go and smooth things over — that's a good girl.

ANNE   Very well, I'll tell Marilla as soon as she comes back that I've repented.

MATTHEW   That's right — that's right, Anne. But don't tell Marilla I said anything about it. She might think I was putting my oar in and I promised not to do that.

ANNE   Wild horses won't drag the secret from me.

MARILLA   *(off)* Anne are you in the kitchen?

ANNE   Yes, Marilla.

MARILLA   *(enters)* Well, why are you down here?

ANNE   I came to tell you I'm sorry I lost my temper and said rude things, and I'm willing to apologize.

MARILLA   Very well. I'll take you down to Rachel's place right away, before she spreads the story all over Avonlea.

> *ANNE suddenly goes from dejected to radiant.*

MARILLA   What are you thinking of, Anne?

ANNE   I'm imagining out what I must say to Mrs. Lynde.

> *Music bridges to next scene.*

Act One, Scene Nine

RACHEL's Front Porch.
RACHEL enters carrying a wicker chair. She
is putting her summer furniture on the porch.
GILBERT, RUBY, JOSIE and DIANA play a
game that follows the lyrics to This Pretty
Little Girl of Mine. *All the gilrs want to kiss*
GILBERT.

ALL   See this pretty little girl of mine
She brought me a penny and a bottle of wine
A bottle of wine and a penny too
To see what my little girl can do

GIRLS   Down on the carpet you must kneel

RACHEL   Gilbert!

GIRLS   While the grass grows high and green
Stand up straight up on your feet
And choose the very one that you love sweet

RACHEL   Gilbert Blythe!

GIRLS   Now you are married I wish you joy
First to a girl and second to a boy
Seven years after seven years to come
To kneel on the carpet, kiss and be done

DIANA   Josie, it's my turn.

As ANNE and MARILLA approach. The
children stop playing and watch. As she walks
toward RACHEL, ANNE's radiance
vanishes. Mournful penitence on every feature.

She walks up to RACHEL and goes down on her knees and holds out her hands beseechingly. The girls don't know what to think and whisper back and forth.

ANNE

Oh, Mrs. Lynde, I am so extremely sorry. I could never express all my sorrow, no, not if I used up a whole dictionary. You must just imagine it. I behaved terribly to you and I've disgraced my dear friends, Matthew and Marilla, who have let me stay at Green Gables although I'm not a boy. I am dreadfully wicked. Every word you said was true. My hair is red and I'm freckled and skinny and ugly. Everything I said was true as well, but I should never have said it except for my unquenchable temper. Oh, Mrs. Lynde, please, please, forgive me. If you refuse, it will be a lifelong sorrow on a poor little orphan girl.

RACHEL

There, there, get up, child. Of course I forgive you.

ANNE

Oh thank you. Thank you forever!

RACHEL

Now, now, I was a little too hard on you, anyway. But I'm such an outspoken person. You just mustn't mind me, that's what. It can't be denied your hair is terrible red but I knew a girl once — went to school with her, in fact — whose hair was as red as yours, but when she grew up it darkened to a real handsome auburn. I wouldn't be a mite surprised if yours did, too — not a mite.

ANNE

Oh, Mrs. Lynde! You have given me hope. I could endure anything if I only thought my hair would be a handsome auburn when I grew up. I shall always feel that you are a benefactor.

RACHEL

(to MARILLA) She's a real odd little thing, Marilla, but there is something taking about her after all. On the whole, Marilla, I kind of

like her. Who would fancy some raspberry cordial?

ANNE   Raspberry cordial. In my whole life I've never had something so appealing.

RACHEL   It won't take a moment.

            RACHEL exits to get the cordial. The girls go back to their skipping.

ANNE   *(proudly)* I apologized pretty thoroughly, didn't I?

MARILLA   You did it thoroughly enough, all right.

ANNE   It gives you a lovely, comfortable feeling to apologize and be forgiven, doesn't it?

MARILLA   I suppose it does.

ANNE   I'll not talk any more just now, Marilla.

MARILLA   Thanks be to goodness for that.

ANNE   Except... Marilla, do you think that I shall ever have a bosom friend in Avonlea?

            RACHEL comes on with the cordial.

MARILLA   A— a what kind of friend?

ANNE   A bosom friend — an intimate friend, you know — a really kindred spirit to whom I can confide my inmost soul. So many of my loveliest dreams have come true all at once that perhaps this one will, too. Do you think it's possible, Mrs. Lynde?

RACHEL   Well, I suppose so. Diana Barry lives right near you over at Orchard Slope and she's about your age.

ANNE   What's she like? Her hair isn't red, is it?

MARILLA	See for yourself, girl. That's her right there.
RACHEL	Diana! Diana Barry come over here, girl!
	The girls stop skipping and watch as DIANA crosses to RACHEL's porch.
DIANA	Yes, Mrs. Lynde?
RACHEL	Diana, this is Anne Shirley who has moved to Green Gables. As you're to be neighbours, you should probably be introduced and there's no time like the present.
ANNE	Hello, Diana.
DIANA	Hello, Anne.
JOSIE	Diana! We're going to my place for tea! Are you coming?
DIANA	Ah... ah... I've got to go.
	DIANA starts to leave.
ANNE	Do you play in the woods!
DIANA	Pardon?
ANNE	The woods between your farm and Green Gables.
DIANA	I've been playing there since I was a baby.
ANNE	They're haunted you know.
DIANA	They are!
ANNE	Well, I'm just pretending they're haunted although perhaps I shouldn't because my imagination is so well-honed I'm sure in no time I'll be seeing the ghost of a mysterious woman walking on the bridge over the lake of shining waters or a child crying by the brook

for her long lost mother.

DIANA   That sounds just like something right out of a
            book.

ANNE   It does?

JOSIE   Diana!

DIANA   I have to go.

ANNE   Oh, yes I suppose you must, but I'm sure I'll see
            you again soon. Tomorrow?

DIANA   I can't tomorrow — my mother is taking me to
            Charlottetown. I'm supposed to spend most of
            the summer with my Aunt.

ANNE   You are?

            *JOSIE tries to take DIANA's hand and lead
            her away. DIANA pulls her hand away.
            JOSIE is amazed and hurt.*

DIANA   Yes, Mother says it will be an education to
            spend the summer in town.

ANNE   Well then... I guess we'll meet again when
            school starts.

JOSIE   Diana!!!

DIANA   I hope so. Bye!

            DIANA runs to the other girls.

ANNE   Oh, I'm so glad she's pretty. Next to being
            beautiful oneself — and that's impossible in
            my case — it would be best to have a beautiful
            bosom friend.

RACHEL   I suppose so, now Marilla, come and see how
            the new quilt is coming along. And you come
            too, Anne. I am famous for my quilts.

*ANNE and MARILLA follow RACHEL
inside.*

ANNE   Oh, Marilla, I think she might truly become
my bosom friend, don't you?

A beat. Lights shift.

Act One, Scene Ten

RACHEL's Front Porch.
GILBERT enters with a basket of apples and crosses the stage towards RACHEL's.

GILBERT   Mrs. Lynde?

RACHEL comes out of her house wearing a shawl.

RACHEL   Good afternoon, Gilbert.

GILBERT   My father sent some apples.

RACHEL   Thank you, Gilbert. How are your prospects for harvest?

GILBERT   Fair to middlin', ma'am.

RACHEL   Good, good. I saw Diana Barry today, fresh back from Charlottetown.

GILBERT   Yes, ma'am.

RACHEL   And school starts tomorrow! Fall must truly be upon us.

GILBERT   Yes, ma'am, do you want some help taking in your furniture?

RACHEL   Gilbert Blythe, you're getting to be quite the young gentleman.

Music bridge to the next scene.

Act One, Scene Eleven

Green Gables.
MARILLA is rummaging around the kitchen
looking for something. She's in an agitated
state. Finally she sits down, wraps herself in
her shawl and rubs her head, indicating one
of her headaches. ANNE comes rushing in.

ANNE   Oh, Marilla, I have been having such an
elegant time! I was...

MARILLA   What time did I tell you to be home, Anne?

ANNE   Two o'clock — but—

MARILLA   Yes, I told you to come at two o'clock. And it's
a quarter to three. When I tell you to come in
at a certain time, I mean that time and not
half an hour later.

ANNE   I am sorry, Marilla, but I was pretending I was
Lady Cordelia Fitzgerald trapped in my castle
by the evil Baron de Mornay who...

MARILLA   Oh, do give me a moment's peace so I can
think, child.

ANNE   What's the matter, Marilla?

MARILLA   I can't seem to find my mother's brooch. I
thought I stuck it in my pincushion when I
came home from church this morning, but I
can't find it anywhere. Did you see anything of
it?

ANNE   I— I saw it after church. I was passing your
door when I saw it on the cushion, so I went in
to look at it.

MARILLA   Did you touch it?

ANNE   Y-e-e-s, I took it up and I pinned it on just to see
            how it would look.

MARILLA   You shouldn't have gone into my room in the
            first place and you shouldn't have touched a
            brooch that didn't belong to you in the second.
            Where did you put it?

ANNE   I put it back on the bureau. I didn't think about
            its being wrong to go in and try on the brooch,
            Marilla, but I see now that it was and I'll
            never do it again. That's one good thing about
            me. I never do the same naughty thing twice.

MARILLA   Anne, the brooch is gone. Tell me the truth.
            Did you take it out and lose it?

ANNE   No, I never took the brooch out of your room
            and that is the truth, if I was to be led to the
            block for it — although I'm not very certain
            what a block is. So there, Marilla.

MATTHEW   *(enters)* Well, I checked in the buggy. You're
            sure it hasn't fell down behind the bureau?

MARILLA   *(to MATTHEW)* I've looked in every crack and
            cranny, moved the bureau and taken out the
            drawers and... *(to ANNE)* Slyness and
            untruthfulness — that's what you are
            displaying, Anne Shirley.

ANNE   I didn't take the brooch!

MARILLA   You must have taken it! I went up to get my
            shawl and the brooch was gone, and you were
            the last one in the room. It's a fearful
            responsibility to have a child in your house
            who is a thief!

MATTHEW   Marilla, there should be allowances made. You
            said yourself, she's never had any bringing up.

MARILLA   Well, she's having it now.

MATTHEW   I think—

MARILLA   Who's bringing this child up, Matthew, you or me?

MATTHEW   Well, now, you.

MARILLA   Don't interfere then.

MATTHEW   Well now, I ain't interfering. It ain't interfering to have your own opinion. And my opinion is that Anne is no thief!

MARILLA   Well, the brooch is gone and she took it, so what would you call her then!

ANNE   All right then! I took the brooch!

I took it just as you said. I didn't mean to take it when I went in. But it looked so beautiful when I pinned it on my breast that I was overcome by an irresistible temptation. I knew it would be so much easier to imagine I was the Lady Cordelia if I wore a real amethyst brooch, so, I took it and when I was going over the bridge across the Lake of Shining Waters I took it off because.... Oh, how it did shine in the sunlight! And then, when I was leaning over the bridge, it just slipped through my fingers — so — and went down-down-down, and sank forevermore beneath the Lake of Shining Waters. And that's the best I can do!

MARILLA   Anne, you are the very wickedest girl I ever heard of.

ANNE   I am and it's your duty to punish me, Marilla. Just so long as I have been thoroughly punished before school starts tomorrow. I'm so looking forward to meeting Diana again and making her my bosom friend.

MARILLA	What makes you think that Mrs. Barry will allow her daughter to become friends with a common thief!
ANNE	Oh, no, oh Marilla, you can't tell Mrs. Barry I stole your brooch. Matthew — she can't!
MATTHEW	Well now, Anne you shouldn't have taken the brooch, but I'm sure you didn't mean it...
MARILLA	Matthew Cuthbert, I'm amazed at you! She doesn't appear to realize how wicked she's been at all and you don't seem to realize it, neither.

> *MARILLA pulls on her shawl and is about to leave, when MATTHEW stops her and points to the shawl.*

MATTHEW	Marilla Cuthbert!
ANNE	Oh!
MARILLA	What are you pointing at with such a... smile on your face, Matthew?
MATTHEW	That there is your brooch hanging on your shawl.

> *MARILLA picks the brooch off the shawl.*

MARILLA	Anne, what is all this rigmarole about!
ANNE	I'm sorry, Marilla, but I just did like Matthew told me I should do with Mrs. Lynde.
MARILLA	Like Matthew told you?
ANNE	He said, "Just sort of smooth it over..."
MATTHEW	Anne, you do beat all!
MARILLA	Matthew, you've been putting your oar in.

ANNE   It's not his fault, Marilla. It just happened is
            all.

MARILLA   But Anne, it wasn't right for you to confess to a
            thing you hadn't done.

ANNE   But I could tell you would never believe me.
            And why should you believe me? I'm just an
            orphan girl and nobody knows what I could do.

MARILLA   *(pause)* Forgive me, Anne. You are right. I
            believed you were a thief because of what I
            have heard said of orphans, not because of
            what I knew to be true about you. I promise
            never to mistrust you anymore if you'll just
            forgive me.

ANNE   Of course I forgive you. I would forgive you
            both anything. You are my saviors.

            Music bridge to next scene.

Act One, Scene Twelve

The Woods/Schoolyard.
JOSIE and RUBY come running on laughing.

RUBY   Liar, liar, pants on fire!

JOSIE   It's true. It's true!

RUBY   I don't believe you for a minute, Josie Pye.

            DIANA enters.

JOSIE   Jealous, jealous, jealous. *(seeing DIANA)* Diana, have you heard?

DIANA   What?

JOSIE   Never mind.

DIANA   What?

            JOSIE zips her lips.

DIANA   What? *(no reply)* Josie!

RUBY   Josie says she went by the school early and she and Gilbert are written up. There's a 'big Take Notice' on the front porch: "Gilbert loves Josie."

JOSIE   I can't believe it.

RUBY   Neither can I.

DIANA   You and Gilbert Blythe. I could never resist Gilbert Blythe.

            They giggle as, unseen by JOSIE, GILBERT

| | *storms on and pulls her hair.* |
| JOSIE | Oh, Gilbert! |

JOSIE squeals, steals his hat and runs off. He follows.

RUBY run off after them. After a moment ANNE rushes on.

| ANNE | Oh Diana, I am so sorry I am late. It is such a difficult thing to decide what one should wear to school on the first day when none of your dresses have puffs and they're all so terribly plain and... and Marilla said I must be on my very best behavior as your mother is so very strict and respectable and religious and expects the same of all her daughters, especially you, and oh, I am starting off so terribly. I will try again. How are you, Diana? |

| DIANA | Fine, Anne. How are you? |

| ANNE | I am well in body although considerably rumpled in spirit, thank you. There wasn't anything startling in that, was there? Marilla says I say the most startling things and your mother wouldn't approve. |

| DIANA | My mother doesn't approve of anything. She doesn't even approve of me reading and I love books. |

| ANNE | *(almost in a whisper)* Oh, Diana, it's true, you do love books? |

| DIANA | More than anything. |

| ANNE | Oh, this is too wonderful, so do I! Books are the very windows of the imagination. I get so many of my best ideas from books. |

| DIANA | You do? |

| ANNE | Oh, yes, for instance; I think we should call |

| | this path Lover's Lane. |
| DIANA | Lover's Lane? |

| ANNE | Not that lovers ever really walk there, but Diana, I am reading a perfectly magnificent book and there's a Lover's Lane in it. So, we ought to have one, too. |

| DIANA | It's a very pretty name, so romantic. |

| ANNE | Yes, it is, isn't it. |

| DIANA | *(pointing)* There are millions of violets down there, too. |

| ANNE | Oh Diana, it takes away my breath. I think we should call this part of our walk Violet Vale. |

| DIANA | Violet Vale. It's like poetry. I never saw the beat of you for hitting on fancy names for places, Anne. It's must be nice to be clever at something, isn't it? |

| ANNE | But Diana, you can name places, too. What's this path we're turning on to called? |

| DIANA | I don't know...The Birch Path? |

| ANNE | The Birch Path. You see that's perfect. |

| DIANA | But I'm sure you could have found something more poetical than plain "Birch Path." Anybody can think of a name like that. |

| ANNE | But Diana, your Birch Path is one of the prettiest places in the world. Listen to the laugh of wind in the trees overhead. |

| DIANA | Anne Shirley, I think you are one of the.... keenest people I have ever met. |

| ANNE | Oh, Diana, do you mean it? Do you really mean it? |

DIANA   I do. You're keen and... and... when we get to
          school I'm going to ask if we can sit together...
          if you'd like.

ANNE   I'd love it! Oh Diana, do you think you could
          be my bosom friend?

DIANA   Why, I guess so.

ANNE   You will? You'll swear to be my friend forever
          and ever?

DIANA   You want me to swear! My mother says it is
          dreadfully wicked to swear!

ANNE   Oh, no. No, my kind of swearing isn't wicked.
          It just means making a solemn promise that
          will last forever and ever.

DIANA   Oh. Well ... how do you do it?

ANNE   *(gravely)* We must join hands. It ought to be
          over running water but we'll just imagine this
          path is running water. I'll repeat the oath
          first. I solemnly swear to be faithful to my
          bosom friend, Diana Barry, as long as the sun
          and moon shall endure. Now, you say it and
          put my name in.

DIANA   *(laughs)* I solemnly swear to be faithful to my
          bosom friend, Anne, as long as the sun and moon
          shall endure.

ANNE   That's... magical! I can imagine no better day
          to be starting at school. It is my intention to be
          the best scholar in Avonlea and to reach the
          very head of my class.

DIANA   That will be hard to do, Anne, because of
          Gilbert Blithe.

ANNE   Who is Gilbert Blythe?

DIANA   He is the smartest, most handsome boy in all
            of Avonlea and every girl in school is mad for
            him, but he teases us all something terrible.
            He just torments our lives out.

            *JOSIE, RUBY and GILBERT come running
            on. JOSIE has GILBERT's hat.*

JOSIE   Monkey in the middle playing on a fiddle.

GILBERT   Josie, give me my hat!

JOSIE   *(throws hat to RUBY)* Ruby!

RUBY   *(catches hat)* Oh, Gilbert!

RUBY   *(throws hat to JOSIE)* Josie.

JOSIE   *(catches hat)* Monkey in the middle.

GILBERT   Josie, give my hat and I'll give you a smooch.

            *JOSIE gives GILBERT the hat. Waits for her
            kiss.*

GILBERT   I'd rather kiss a ... a tommy cod.

JOSIE   Oh, Gilbert!

            *RUBY and JOSIE see DIANA and break
            away from the game, running up to them.*

JOSIE   You're Anne, aren't you?

ANNE   That's right, I am.

RUBY   I'm Ruby. And that's Josie. We're classmates.
            Do you sing?

ANNE   Well I...

RUBY   Because we have concerts on Fridays.

ANNE   Oh, that is grand. I do love to vocalize.

JOSIE   Good , they say "music hath charms to soothe
               the savage beast." *(the girls giggle)*

RUBY   Oh Josie, you are such a pest. She's just saying
               that because we know you had that terrible
               blowout with Mrs. Lynde and that is why you
               had to apologize to her that day we all saw
               you at the start of the summer.

ANNE   Well, I did lose my temper with her, but I
               haven't lost my temper ever since and I don't
               suppose I ever will again. Do you sing, Josie?

JOSIE   No, I hate singing.

RUBY   You hate everything, Josie. Anyway, Anne,
               pleased to meet you, I'm sure.

ANNE   And I'm honoured to meet you.

               She solemnly shakes hands with RUBY.
               JOSIE snickers. GILBERT catches ANNE's
               eye and winks. She looks away.

ANNE   Who is that rude boy?

JOSIE   That's Gilbert Blythe.

DIANA   Don't you think Gilbert's handsome?

ANNE   I think your Gilbert Blythe is handsome but I
               think he's very bold. It isn't good manners to
               wink at a strange girl.

               She looks at GILBERT. He winks. She looks
               away. He crosses to her.

GILBERT   Hi there.

               He offers his hand and ANNE is about to take
               it when he pulls her braids.

GILBERT   Carrots!

ANNE   You mean, hateful boy! How dare you!

            ANNE cracks her slate over GILBERT's head.

GIRLS   Oh!

ANNE   This is the end of all things.

            End of Act One.

Act Two, Scene One

Green Gables / In Front of RACHEL's House.
RACHEL, DIANA and JOSIE stand talking
in front of RACHEL's. Simultaneously we see
ANNE rush into the house. ANNE pulls a
vial of something out of her pocket. She looks
at the instructions.

DIANA   I told her, "You mustn't mind Gilbert making fun of your hair."

JOSIE   Why, he makes fun of all the girls.

DIANA   I told her that. I said, "He calls me a crow because my hair is so black."

RUBY   And what did she say?

DIANA   "There's a great deal of difference between being called a crow and being called carrots."

ANNE puts on an apron, pours hot water into
a basin, adds the contents of the vial and
carries the basin upstairs.

RUBY   Gilbert whispered to her and handed her something in class, didn't he?

DIANA   Uh huh.

RUBY   What did he say?

DIANA   He said he was sorry and, "Don't be mad for keeps".

JOSIE   But what did he give her?

DIANA   A "Love Heart".

JOSIE   A "Love Heart".

DIANA   That's right and it said, "You are sweet."

RUBY   Oh, I could never resist Gilbert Blythe.

JOSIE   What did she do then?

DIANA   She dropped the candy on the ground and
               stepped on it.

JOSIE
& RUBY   Oh!!!

DIANA   She said "Gilbert Blythe has hurt my feelings
               excruciatingly and I shall never speak to him
               again."

JOSIE   Well, I must say I admire her strength.

RUBY   I could never resist Gilbert Blythe.

DIANA   She told me, "The iron has entered my soul".

               Offstage, ANNE is looking at the results of
               her handiwork. We hear a series of gasps
               building to a horrified scream.

Act Two, Scene Two

Green Gables.
The kitchen is empty. Low light. MARILLA
enters.

MARILLA   Anne! You've let the fire go out and tea was to
be ready at five o'clock! Matthew will be
home soon and there's nothing for him!

MARILLA grimly starts to make tea.

MARILLA   Gadding off somewhere with Diana Barry, I
suppose, and never thinking once about the
time or her duties. Matthew's tea will be late.

ANNE appears, hiding in the shadows with a
towel over her head.

ANNE   I'm sorry, Marilla and I would have made tea,
but...

MARILLA   Anne? What's the matter?

MARILLA moves towards ANNE.

ANNE   I'm in the depths of despair and I don't
suppose I'll ever go to school again.

MARILLA   Anne Shirley, come into this room this minute
and tell me. This minute, I say.

ANNE steps into the light. Her hair is green.

MARILLA   Anne Shirley, what have you done to your
hair? Why, it's GREEN!

ANNE   I thought nothing could be as bad as red hair.
But now I know it's ten times worse to have

green hair. Oh, Marilla, you little know how utterly wretched I am.

MARILLA   I little know how you got into this fix, but I mean to find out. Just what have you done to your hair?

ANNE   I dyed it.

MARILLA   Dyed your hair green?

ANNE   I didn't mean to dye it green, Marilla. The bottle said it would turn my hair a beautiful raven black.

MARILLA   Anne Shirley, didn't you know dyeing your hair was a wicked thing to do?

ANNE   Oh, Marilla, when I saw the dreadful colour it turned my hair, I knew it was, I can tell you. And I've been repenting ever since.

MARILLA   Well, I hope you'll repent to good purpose and that you've got your eyes opened to where your vanity has led you.

Examining ANNE's hair.

ANNIE   Oh, Marilla, I can never live this down. People will think I am not respectable. And how Josie Pye will laugh! Marilla, I *cannot* face Josie Pye. I am the unhappiest girl in Prince Edward Island. What shall I do?

MARILLA   That is fast dye if ever there was any. Your hair must be cut off. There is no other way. You can't go out with it looking like that.

MARILLA gets the scissors and hands them to ANNE who holds them point up like a sacrificial dagger.

ANNIE   The girls in books lose their hair in fevers or sell it to get money for some good deed, not because they've dyed it green. I'm going to weep all the time you're cutting it off, if it won't interfere.

ANNE leads MARILLA off, scissors held high.

I never thought I was vain about my hair, of all things, but now I know I was, in spite of its being red, because it was so long and thick and curly. I expect something will happen to my nose next.

They exit. Musical bridge to next scene.

Act Two, Scene Three

The School.
JOSIE comes on with a note in her hand. She
looks around and then tacks it up on the
school house door. She runs off. GILBERT
walks on, sees the notice and pulls it off the
door.

GILBERT "Take Notice, Gilbert and Josie". Josie! Josie
Pye!

He crumples it up and exits.

Act Two, Scene Four

Green Gables.
The older DIANA, RUBY, RACHEL, and
MATTHEW all sit in the parlour laughing as
they tell stories.

RACHEL She told Marilla, "I'll never, never look at
myself again until my hair grows." Then she
said,

RACHEL
DIANA
& RUBY "Yes, I will, too!"

RACHEL "I'll do penance for being wicked that way. I'll
look at myself every day and see how ugly I
am. And I won't try to imagine it away,
either."

RUBY   And Marilla had to let her stay at home until
            it grew in! Didn't you Marilla?

MARILLA   *(enters the parlour with a fresh tray of sweets)*
            Well, mercy, I couldn't let her out looking like
            a badly shorn, shamrock-shaded sheep, could
            I?

RACHEL   What a girl she was for making mistakes!
            Always getting into scrapes.

MARILLA   And she'd would always insist, "I must be
            improving because I must be running out of new
            mistakes to make."

MATTHEW   She did suffer terrible over her hair and
            freckles. Didn't you, Anne!

ANNE   *(enters)* I certainly did, but my freckles are
            finally gone, and people are nice enough to tell
            me my hair is auburn now.

DIANA   Except for yesterday — Josie Pye told her she
            thought it's redder than ever and asked if
            people who have red hair ever really get used
            to having it.

MARILLA   Now, isn't that just perfect Pye.

ANNE   I've made what I would once have called a
            heroic effort to like her, but Josie Pye just won't
            be liked. And I believe I've known that since
            the first day we ever met.

RACHEL   Now Anne, Josie is a Pye, so she can't help
            being disagreeable.

MARILLA   I suppose people of that kind serve some useful
            purpose in society, but I must say I don't know
            what it is any more than I know the use of
            thistles.

RACHEL   Ruby, did you hear anything in Charlottetown
            about the Abbey Bank?

RUBY   I heard it was shaky. Why?

RACHEL   Because Marilla and Matthew have all their savings in that bank — every penny. If the bank fails, they'll be ruined.

MATTHEW   Old Mr. Abbey was a great friend of father's. A bank with him at the head of it was good enough for anybody.

RACHEL   He is a very old man — his nephews are really at the head of the institution. You should get them to draw their money out of there, Anne, right now.

MATTHEW   Well now, Rachel, I read in the paper just yesterday that the bank was all right.

RACHEL   There's no talking to you, Matthew Cuthbert, and there never has been.

MATTHEW   That may be true, but a man's got a right to manage his affairs without the neighbours meddling. *(embarrassed by his outburst)* Ah, I best see to that broken fence in the meadow. Morning's half gone.

              MATTHEW exits rubbing his left arm — heart pain.

DIANA   Ah, well... we should be off too, I suppose.

RACHEL   Yes, I've promised Ruby's mother a visit for lunch.

              RACHEL stands to go. RUBY and DIANA follow suit.

RUBY   Thank you for tea, Marilla. See you soon, Anne. *(going off)* Diana, have you heard that Mr. Brown, that handsome teacher from the school at White Sands...

RACHEL   ...has resigned! And we'll say no more about
              that!

              ANNE talks softly to MARILLA.

ANNE   Marilla, is Matthew quite well?

MARILLA   He's had some bad spells with his heart this
              spring. I've been real worried about him, but he
              won't spare himself a mite.

ANNE   We have to get him to rest.

MARILLA   Maybe he will pick up now you're home. You
              always cheer him up.

ANNE   You are not looking as well yourself as I'd like
              to see you, Marilla.

MARILLA   Oh, I'm fine.

ANNE   No, you look tired. It's your headaches. Are
              they getting worse?

MARILLA   It's nothing new, and nothing for you to worry
              about. *(changing the subject)* You were right
              surprised to hear Gilbert Blythe was going to
              teach, weren't you?

ANNE   Yes. I confess I was. I still don't know what to
              think about him not going on.

MARILLA   Oh, the rivalry between you two! *(laughs)* And
              what a nice-looking fellow he is. You know,
              people used to call Gilbert's father my beau.

ANNE   Oh, Marilla — and what happened?

MARILLA   We had a quarrel. I wouldn't forgive him
              when he asked me to. I meant to, later on, but I
              was sulky and angry and I wanted to punish
              him first. He never came back. *(pause)* You
              know, I've always kind of wished I'd forgiven
              him when I had the chance.

Act Two, Scene Five

A small landing on the stream leading to the Lake of Shining Waters. DIANA, JOSIE and RUBY stand beside a small boat in "dress up" versions of medieval garb.

RUBY   He's sweet on her. There is no doubt about it whatsoever.

JOSIE   Ruby Gillis, you are the stupidest girl in all of Avonlea. Gilbert Blythe and Anne Shirley are the biggest of rivals.

DIANA   It's true. Anne has vowed eternal enmity to Gilbert Blythe.

RUBY   I didn't say *she* liked him. I said *he* was sweet on her.

DIANA   The stream's right high for the fall, isn't it?

JOSIE   All the better. It's more dramatic. *(to RUBY)* Then who wrote Gilbert and me up at school?

RUBY   I thought you did that yourself, Josie — same as last time.

JOSIE   You are a hateful little child, Ruby Gillis. Absolutely hateful.

DIANA   I could never resist Gilbert — ever. The boat's leaky, but I bailed it out so it should be fine.

RUBY   Rachel Lynde says Gilbert and Anne are a match made in heaven because Gilbert is the only boy in school smart enough to keep up with her.

JOSIE   Well, being smart isn't everything, you know. And Gilbert Blythe isn't the sort of fellow to get himself involved with some... some... bad-tempered orphan.

DIANA   Josie Pye, don't you dare say that about Anne!

JOSIE   Well it's true. You both fawn over her since she started The Story Club but that's just because she's the only one with the imagination to think up a story and I don't suppose that's so hard to do when you're brought up in an orphanage where they teach you to lie.

DIANA   You take that back or I'll...

ANNE enters dressed in a knight's cape with a wooden spoon sword.

ANNE   Good 'morrow, fair maidens!

RUBY   Shuss... here she comes.

JOSIE   Why Anne, we were just talking about you!

ANNE   You were?

JOSIE   Yes. It was such a good idea to act out "Elaine." We're all so terribly excited about it.

RUBY   It will be so much fun.

ANNE   It will be, won't it! But, first we must call The Story Club to order. Diana, I believe you are the current secretary?

DIANA   You are hateful, Josie Pye and I hereby call this meeting of The Story Club opened. Anne Shirley, The Story Girl, in the Chair.

ANNE   Thank you, Diana. The only business before The Story Club this week concerns a motion made last week that at our next meeting, we would enact the tragic tale of "Elaine of Camelot". I open the floor to discussion.

RUBY   Good. Who's going to play Elaine?

DIANA   I think it should be...

JOSIE   No Diana, I can't. Of course, it would be romantic to do it but I know I'd be popping up every minute or so to see where I was and that would spoil the effect.

              JOSIE gets in the boat.

DIANA   I was going to say Anne is the only one of us with the imagination to play Elaine.

ANNE   Oh no, I couldn't be Elaine, it's ridiculous. Ruby ought to do it because she has such lovely long golden hair.

RUBY   Oh no, Anne, I couldn't. I don't mind floating down when there's two or three of us in the boat and we can sit up. It's fun then. But to lie down and pretend I was dead — I'd die of fright.

ANNE   But a red-haired person cannot play Elaine. Bright red hair is just too unattractive!

DIANA   But your hair is ever so much darker than it used to be before you cut it.

ANNE   Oh, do you really think so? I've sometimes thought it was myself — but I never dared to ask anyone for fear she would tell me it wasn't. Do you think it could be called auburn now, Diana?

DIANA   Yes, and I think it is real pretty.

ANNE   All right then, it's settled. I shall be Elaine.

JOSIE   What?

ANNE looks at the boat.

ANNE   Is this boat quite sound?

JOSIE   No, it leaks.

DIANA   It leaks some, but not all that much. And you
            can bail if you need to.

ANNE   *(whispers)* You do know that I don't swim, don't
            you, Diana?

JOSIE   Well if you're scared...

ANNE   I'm not scared.

JOSIE   Scaredy cat! Scaredy cat!

ANNE   I'm not scared. And I'll prove it.

JOSIE   OK then, prove it.

ANNE   Very well, I shall.

            *JOSIE jumps out. ANNE jumps in, laying
            down and folding her hands over her breast.*

DIANA   Oh, she does look really dead.

RUBY   It makes me feel frightened. Do you suppose
            it's really right to act like this? Mrs. Lynde
            says that all play-acting is abominably
            wicked.

ANNE   Ruby, you shouldn't talk about Mrs. Lynde. It
            spoils the effect because this is hundreds of
            years before Mrs. Lynde was born.

JOSIE   Shuss. It's silly for Elaine to be talking when
            she's dead.

            ANNE lays back, pretending to be dead.

JOSIE

Good, now we will begin. We must kiss her quiet brow and you say, "Sister, farewell forever. Farewell, sweet sister." Both of you — as sorrowfully as you possibly can.

They kiss her brow.

DIANA

Sister, farewell forever. Farewell, sweet sister...

RUBY

Sister, farewell forever. Farewell... Oh... I can't...

JOSIE

Oh, just push the boat off.

DIANA

We'll meet you below the bridge.

They push off the boat. JOSIE stands with the oars. The girls sing a fragment of The Song of Love and Death, *from Tennyson's "Idylls of The King". ANNE drifts downstream.*

TRIO

Sweet is true love though given in vain, in vain
And sweet is death who puts end to pain
O Love, if death be sweeter, let me die.

ANNE drifts along enjoying the romance of her situation and singing with the girls, but then she sits up, pulls a soaking edge of the shawl out of the boat and wrings it out.

ANNE

I'm leaking. No, I'm sinking! Where are the oars? *(kneels and prays)* Dear God, please take me close to a piling on the bridge and I'll do the rest. Dear God, please take me close to a piling and I'll do the rest. Dear God, please take me close to a piling and I'll do the rest.

Finally the boat drifts close enough to the bridge for ANNE to leap to a piling. She clings to the piling.

ANNE   Sweet is true love though given in vain, in
              vain
              And sweet is death who puts end to pain

                        GILBERT, who has been fishing nearby,
                        comes swaggering up.

GILBERT   Anne Shirley! What in the world are you
              doing?

ANNE   We were re-enacting "Elaine of Camelot" and I
              was playing Elaine so had to drift down to
              Camelot in a funeral barge. But it started to
              sink.

GILBERT   So, you had to float to Camelot in a leaky
              boat?

ANNE   I did not expect it to sink, Gilbert.

GILBERT   No, I suppose not. Well, come on take my
              hand!

ANNE   I am expecting help at any moment.

GILBERT   Don't be silly, Anne. Take my hand and jump.

                        Without waiting for an answer he extends his
                        hand. ANNE, clinging to GILBERT Blythe's
                        hand, jumps to shore twisting her ankle.

ANNE   Ow!!!

GILBERT   Are you all right?

ANNE   Fine. I've twisted my ankle is all.

GILBERT   Are you sure?

ANNE   Positive. Thank you for your assistance, Mr.
              Blythe.

GILBERT   You're welcome... Anne, look here. Can't we be
              good friends? I'm awfully sorry I made fun of

your hair that time. I didn't mean to vex you and I only meant it for a joke. Besides, it's so long ago. I think your hair is awfully pretty now — honest I do. *(offers her hand)* Let's be friends

ANNE Oh, Gilbert, I... Gilbert, you called me "carrots".

GILBERT I know but—

ANNE You disgraced me in front of the whole school.

GILBERT It was just a—

ANNE On my first day!

GILBERT I was just being friendly, Anne. The other girls like to be teased.

ANNE Well, I am not "other girls".

GILBERT But Anne—

ANNE No, I shall never be friends with you, Gilbert Blythe. I don't want to be!

GILBERT All right! I'll never ask you to be friends again, Anne Shirley. I don't care either!

The girls come rushing up.

DIANA Gilbert, Gilbert we saw the boat drifting, swamped and we thought....

Anne, we thought you were drowned.

RUBY And we felt like murderers because we had made you be Elaine.

JOSIE Yes, how did you escape?

ANNE I... I managed to jump on to a bridge piling and... Gilbert, he...

RUBY   Gilbert saved you!

DIANA   Oh, Gilbert, how splendid of you!

RUBY   Why, it's so romantic!

JOSIE   I suppose she'll have to speak to you now.

ANNE   I won't, and I don't want ever to hear the word 'romantic' again.

> *ANNE stamps her foot. Her ankle gives out. She yelps in pain and faints. As she falls GILBERT sweeps her into his arms.*

DIANA   She's fainted!

RUBY   Oh, Gilbert.

GILBERT   It will be all right. She's just twisted her ankle. I'll carry her home.

> *GILBERT carries ANNE off.*

RUBY   *(to JOSIE)* Told you so. It's love.

> *JOSIE exits. RUBY and DIANA begin to sing the song again, as they clear the stage.*

RUBY
& DIANA   Sweet is true love though given in vain, in vain
And sweet is death who puts end to pain
O Love, if death be sweeter, let me die.

Act Two, Scene Six

Green Gables.
Lights up on the parlour. JOSIE sits at the
organ (or piano) playing The Island Hymn
and trying to make the lyrics fit the tune.

JOSIE   *(sings)* Fair Island of the sea,
We raise our song to thee,
The bright and blest
(losing the scansion) Loyally now we stand

These words just don't fit the song, Anne.

ANNE   *(in the kitchen)* They do!

JOSIE   As brothers, hand in hand,
And sing God save the land
(losing the scansion) We love the best

They don't, and I've been singing this song
with the real words since I was a mere child,
so I should know.

   ANNE enters the parlour.

ANNE   *(sings so it works)* "We love the best." You just
need to practice.

JOSIE   Well, I'm certainly not going to make a fool of
myself trying to sing these words this
afternoon, just because you wrote them.

ANNE   Oh, I guess you're right. It would sound awful.

   RUBY, DIANA enter dressed in their "good"
   outfits, trying to act like adults.

RUBY & DIANA	*(outside)* Miss Shirley!
	ANNE limps eagerly to greet her friends, shares an excited squeal with them and leads them into the parlour area..
RUBY	Anne. How is your ankle?
ANNE	Very nearly healed, thank you. Marilla says she'll let me go back to school next week.
DIANE	It was very kind of you to invite us to tea.
ANNE	Oh Diana, isn't it exciting! When Marilla told me that I could invite The Story Club to tea all by myself while she went to Ladies Aid, I thought, "How perfectly lovely!" And your mothers let you come! I mean, it proves we're practically grown up! *(pause)* I even asked her if we could use the rosebud spray tea set.
RUBY	The rosebud tea set!
ANNE	She said it was used only for special occasions and I said this was a very special occasion for me and she said her only concern was that the whole event might make me more addle-pated than ever. But she gave us the brown tea set which I believe is even prettier than the rosebud and she said we can have fruitcake and cookies and snaps and...
JOSIE	It isn't good manners to tell your company what you are going to give them to eat.
ANNE	Thank you Josie, you're right. So I won't tell you what she said we could have to drink. Only it begins with an R and a C and it's a bright red colour. I love bright red drinks, don't you?
DIANA	Oh, yes, they taste twice as good as any other colour.

ANNE	At least twice as good. I'm sure you will enjoy it.
JOSIE	Enjoy what?
ANNE	Sorry, it would be bad manners to tell.
RUBY	Oh do tell us, Anne. I hate secrets.
ANNE	It's raspberry cordial! Marilla's famous raspberry cordial.

ANNE limps out of the room.

JOSIE	Raspberry cordial. It's as if she's never had raspberry cordial before. My mother serves it daily.
DIANA	Josie! You are not being a very good guest.
JOSIE	Well, I beg your pardon. I will try and do better.

ANNE returns carrying a tray with a bottle and glasses and pours drinks.

ANNE	Now, please help yourself. I won't have any just now as I have so much to do to get tea prepared.

DIANA looks at its bright-red hue admiringly, and then sips it daintily. JOSIE and RUBY both take sips as well.

DIANA	That's really nice raspberry cordial, Anne.
JOSIE	Oh yes, I didn't know raspberry cordial could taste so good.
ANNE	I'm really glad you like it. Drink as much as you like.

ANNE hurries out. JOSIE sniffs the drink knowingly.

RUBY

This doesn't taste like raspberry cordial at all.

JOSIE

Now, now Ruby we mustn't be bad guests. We'll just have to pretend we like it, won't we, Diana?

DIANA

I think it's delicious.

JOSIE

Of course you do.

> *ANNE re-enters with the tea and puts it down.*

ANNE

It will just take a moment to steep.

JOSIE

There's no rush, not with this delicious cordial at hand. Diana just loves it, don't you, Diana?

DIANA

It's the best I've ever had.

> *She takes a long drink. A pause.*

ANNE

So, Diana? How is your mother?

DIANA

She is very well, thank you. I hope your father's potato crop is good too, Josie.

JOSIE

It is fairly good, thank you.

ANNE

How are things at school?

DIANA

Without you? Awful.

JOSIE

Diana is sitting with me now.

DIANA

Yes, and you squeak the chalk all the time.

RUBY

She does it on purpose too!

JOSIE

Doesn't that just make your blood run cold.

DIANA

Everybody misses you so and wishes you'd come to school again soon, Anne.

RUBY   Even Gilbert Blythe.

ANNE   I won't hear a word about Gilbert Blythe.

DIANA   But Anne, Gilbert just wants to make it up with you.

ANNE   Diana!

          DIANA, a bit intimidated by ANNE's reaction to her comments, takes the bottle from JOSIE and fills her tumbler again.

DIANA   This is the nicest stuff I ever drank. It's ever so much nicer than Mrs. Lynde's, although she brags of hers so much.

ANNE   Marilla is a superior cook.

JOSIE   I'm sure. Is she teaching you?

ANNE   She is trying but, I assure you, it is uphill work. There's so little scope for imagination in cookery.

DIANA   You just have to go by rules.

ANNE   Exactly. The last time I made a cake I forgot to put the flour in. I was thinking the loveliest story about you and me, Diana. You were desperately ill with smallpox and everybody deserted you.

          DIANA takes another drink.

RUBY   Then what happened?

ANNE   I went boldly to her bedside and nursed her back to life and then I took the smallpox and died and Diana planted a rosebush by my grave and watered it with her tears and she never, never forgot the friend of her youth who sacrificed her life for her.

DIANA	Oh, Anne.
ANNE	It was such a pathetic tale that the tears just rained down over my cheeks while I mixed the cake, so, I forgot the flour and the cake was a dismal failure.
DIANA	Flour is so essential to cakes, you know.
ANNE	So I have learned. Why, Diana, what is the matter?"

> *DIANA suddenly stands unsteadily.*

DIANA	I'm — I'm awful sick, I--I--must go right home.
JOSIE	I never heard of company going home without tea.
ANNE	Oh, you mustn't dream of going home without your tea!

> *ANNE rushes to get the tea tray. She returns. It is laden with sweets*

RUBY	Where do you feel bad Diana?
DIANA	I'm awful dizzy and... and...
ANNE	(*putting the tray right under DIANA's nose*) Let me give you a bit of fruitcake and some of the cherry preserves.

> *DIANA covers her mouth and runs out.*
> *ANNE follows. RUBY follows last.*

ANNE	(*off*) Oh, Diana!
JOSIE	What a pity.

> *JOSIE goes to the piano and begins to play*
> *ANNE's song. RUBY enters looking pale.*

JOSIE   Listen Ruby, Anne has written a song
especially for the occasion. It's sheer poetry.

Fair Island of the sea,
We raise our song to thee,
The bright and blest...

RUBY   You are evil, Josie Pye.

JOSIE   More cordial, Ruby?

Musical bridge to next scene.

Act Two, Scene Seven

Green Gables.
ANNE is carefully pinning the amethyst
brooch on MARILLA.

ANNE
It's been three whole months and Mrs. Barry still won't forgive me?

MARILLA
I'm sorry, Anne. If I told her once, I've told her a hundred times it was all my fault.

ANNE
I didn't know you had put out your homemade currant wine.

MARILLA
It was a mistake. But that doesn't change the fact that Diana came home dead drunk. Mrs. Barry does not approve of my homemade currant wine under any circumstances.

ANNE
Diana will be all alone with Minnie Mae tonight and I should be staying with her. I really should and... I'm just overcome with woe. Mrs Barry is never, never going to let Diana play with me again.

MARILLA
I'm sorry, Anne...

ANNE
It's all right, Marilla I have learned from sad experience that sometimes tragedy cannot be avoided but Diana will be in my heart forever. She has sent me a lock of her hair and the most beautiful letter. Please see that they are buried with me, for I don't believe I'll live very long. Perhaps, when she sees me lying cold and dead before her, Mrs. Barry will let Diana come to my funeral.

MARILLA   I don't think there is much fear of your dying
            of grief, Anne, as long as you can talk.

            *Sleigh bells approaching. MARILLA looks out
            the window.*

MARILLA   Well, there's Rachel. Best get on my coat.

ANNE   *(a beat)* It seems like all of Avonlea is going to
            the rally.

MARILLA   I shouldn't be surprised. This is the first time a
            Prime Minister has been down this way in
            winter since Sir John A. MacDonald himself
            and entertainment is terrible scarce in January.
            You and Matthew will be all right on your
            own, won't you, Anne?

ANNE   Yes, I am looking forward to a horribly dull
            night with my geometry book. *(sigh)* But all I
            really want to do is read Diana's last letter
            again and again. She used 'thee' and 'thou' all
            through that letter, Marilla. It was...
            heartbreaking.

MARILLA   Now, don't you worry about that Mrs. Barry,
            Anne, she'll come around eventually.

ANNE   Do you really think so, Marilla?

MARILLA   I know so. Why the Barrys are a far too
            Christian a family to hold a grudge more than
            three or four years.

            ANNE groans as MARILLA exits.

Act Two, Scene Eight

The Barry Kitchen.
A strong winter wind is blowing, and on it
the hint of something else, the gasping breath
of a sick little girl. The coughing gets louder.
A baby's crib sits in the corner near the fire.
DIANA stands in the window waving a
candle.

DIANA   Three flashes. Three flashes, "come immediately — emergency". Please Anne, please come. (*putting down the candle she comforts the baby*) There, there, Minnie Mae. It will be all right. It's warmer in here and... and help is coming.

ANNE   (*rushes in*) Diana! What's the matter.

DIANA   (*off*) Oh, Anne, Minnie Mae is sick, awful bad and... I know I'm forbidden to see you, Anne, but I'm all alone with her and... Anne, I'm so ascared!

ANNE   Let me see her.

ANNE looks in the cradle.

DIANA   She can't breathe, Anne. Is it the croup?

ANNE   It's the croup, all right.

DIANA   I think she's dying!

ANNE   Do you have any ipecac?

DIANA   I don't know.

ANNE   Where do you keep your medicine?

DIANA	In the pantry.
	ANNE disappears into the pantry. DIANA is close to panic.
DIANA	She sounds awful bad, Anne. I had a cousin come down with the croup when she was three and my mother said she was dead before the night was out. "She just coughed out her little soul", that's what my mother said. "And there was nothing anybody could do."
ANNE	Stop it, Diana. Put on your coat and run to Green Gables. Tell Matthew he must go get a doctor.
DIANA	He won't find a doctor. I know. Doctor Blair said he was going to town.
ANNE	He will find a doctor even if he has to drive to Carmody. Hurry.
	DIANA exits. ANNE goes to the cradle and gently spoons some medicine into Minnie Mae. The baby coughs and cries.
ANNE	I know, Minnie. I know — it tastes awful, but you've got to drink it all, every last drop.
	The coughing gets worse. ANNE forces another spoonful down.
ANNE	Oh Minnie, please, please take your medicine. You're sicker than the Hammond twins ever were and this is all I know how to do. I'm afraid too, Minnie.
	ANNE administers another dose and picks her up.
ANNE	There, there now. There, there.
	ANNE paces with the baby as the crying and coughing build and then stop dead.

Act Two, Scene Nine

> *Green Gables.*
> *MARILLA and MATTHEW sit in the kitchen*
> *with DIANA.*

JOSIE   *(off)* Hello! Anybody home?

> *RUBY and JOSIE rush in.*

RUBY   Mrs. Lynde just told us the news! Is it true, Diana?

MARILLA   Shuss, Anne's still sleeping.

DIANA   *(whispered)* It is true. Anne saved Minnie Mae. She saved her, didn't she, Matthew?

MATTHEW   *(whispered)* Yup. The doctor, he told Mr. and Mrs. Barry... *(shyness overtakes him)* Well, he said... ah...

MARILLA   *(whispered)* He said, "That little redheaded girl they have over at Cuthbert's is as smart as they make 'em. I tell you she saved that baby's life."

MATTHEW   *(whispered)* It would have been too late by the time I found the Doc and got him over to Orchard Slope. That's what he said! Ain't she something?

DIANA   *(whispered)* Mother says we can never repay Anne and we are to be good friends again. *(offering a card to RUBY for inspection)* I made a card too.

RUBY

(whispered)"If you love me as I love you
Nothing but death can part us two."

Oh, I think I'm going to cry.

> *JOSIE makes a face and hands her a hanky.*
> *ANNE enters, yawning.*

ANNE

Good morning. What time is it?

MATTHEW

'Bout noon, I guess.

> *Realizing her friends are in the room.*

ANNE

Ruby, Josie... Diana?

DIANA

Mother sent me to thank you. All is forgiven.

RUBY

It's all over town, Anne. Saving Minnie Mae!
You're, you're... like... like Florence Nightingale

ANNE

I'm just lucky Mrs. Hammond had three pairs
of twins after all. If she hadn't, I mightn't
have known what to do. Oh Diana, do you
think the teacher will let us sit together in
school again?

DIANA

I do. *(to JOSIE)* My mother said she must.

JOSIE

Of course she must, don't worry about your
other friends. I'll just sit with Mary Andrews
and hope I don't get warts.

DIANA

Mother says she's going to host an elegant
party when we graduate and you will be the
guest of honour. It will be an elegant tea with
our very best china set out.

ANNE

Nobody ever used their very best china on my
account before.

DIANA

Well, we will and we'll have fruit cake and
pound cake and doughnuts and two kinds of
preserves and everyone will wear their most

elegant gowns, too. Now, Mother wants you to come over and see her so she can thank you personally.

ANNE   May I, Marilla?

MARILLA   Of course. Go along.

ANNE   You see before you a perfectly happy person, Marilla. I'm perfectly happy — yes, in spite of my red hair. Just at present I have a soul above red hair.

              The girls dream of their gowns as they exit.

RUBY   Oh, Josie, a garden party! I know just what I'm going to wear. White organdy. We've got a brand new shipment of dress material in at the store and...

JOSIE   Organdy. That is elegant, Ruby but you'll still have to make it yourself. My father is having a graduation gown made especially for me by the best dressmakers in Charlottetown. In pink damask.

              MATTHEW sits and thinks for a second and then gets out his pipe. MARILLA looks at him and scowls.

MARILLA   You're going to smoke.

              MATTHEW grunts and packs in some tobacco, eventually lighting up. MARILLA opens the windows.

MARILLA   Well then, what is it you're trying to figure out this time?

MATTHEW   Marilla, there is something different about Anne.

MARILLA   Different?

MATTHEW   From the other girls. Not just that she's
               prettier either. Something else. I just can't
               make out what. *(pause)* You know, I suspect
               that Anne is not dressed like the other girls.
               (pause) In fact, the more I think on it, I'm sure
               she isn't. Never since she come to Green Gables.

MARILLA   Anne is dressed very respectably.

MATTHEW   Well now, I don't know. It's her... sleeves I
               think. Her sleeves don't look at all like the
               sleeves the other girls wear. And her dresses
               are all black and brown. Why do you keep her
               so plain, Marilla?

MARILLA   She always has three good, warm, serviceable
               dresses. Anything more would just pamper her
               vanity, Matthew, and she's as vain as a
               peacock now.

MATTHEW   Of course, you know best. But in less than six
               months she'll be graduating school. It would do
               no harm to give the child one pretty dress,
               something like Diana Barry always wears,
               would it?

MARILLA   With big puffed sleeves that take almost as
               much material as a dress itself to make. It
               would be nothing but extravagance.

MATTHEW   I don't know about that. I don't.

               Musical bridge.

Act Two, Scene Ten

The Store.
RUBY enters in an apron and sets up the
Avonlea General store. As she sets up, JOSIE
and DIANA cross the stage together, talking.

JOSIE   Well, I think it's just terrible that your mother
won't let you write the entrance examinations
for Queen's. You're the only one of our whole
set who's not studying for them.

DIANA   I know, it's terrible. Anne is bound to go as
she's at the top of the class.

JOSIE   Except for Gilbert.

DIANA   Along with Gilbert. You know Ruby says Anne
is going to be elected class valedictorian at
commencement.

JOSIE   Yes, I suppose she should be — you can't ever
get her to be quiet, anyway. Why won't your
mother let you come, Diana?

DIANA   Mother says education is wasted on a girl as
our proper sphere is marriage and the home.

JOSIE   Well, of course she's right, but that's all the
more reason to go to Queen's.

DIANA   It is?

JOSIE   I should say so! Why, the only eligible
bachelor in all of Avonlea is Gilbert Blythe
and he's going to Queen's for sure. Who does
your mother think you'll find to wed 'round
here? Moody Spurgeon?

DIANA   *(DIANA shrieks)* Josie, you are a... a torturing
               demon!

JOSIE   Diana and Moody sitting in a tree K-I-S-S-I-N-G!

               *DIANA screams again and runs off, followed
               by JOSIE. They run past MATTHEW, who
               looks at them nervously and then approaches
               the store counter.*

Act Two, Scene Eleven

The Store.

RUBY   What can I do for you this evening, Mr.
Cuthbert?

MATTHEW   Have you any ... any ... any... well now, say,
any garden rakes?

RUBY   Well now, we don't get much call for garden
rakes this early in the year, but I believe we
have one or two left over from the fall. I'll go
and see.

           *MATTHEW talks to himself, rehearsing what
           he has to say. RUBY returns with the rake.*

RUBY   Here you are, Mr. Cuthbert. Anything else
tonight?

MATTHEW   Well now, since you suggest it, I might as well,
take, that is, look at... buy some... some
hayseed.

RUBY   We don't get the hayseed until closer to planting.

MATTHEW   Oh, certainly, certainly. Just as you say.

           *MATTHEW grabs the rake and heads for the
           door. At the threshold he remembers he
           hasn't paid for it and turns miserably back.*

MATTHEW   Now, how much would the rake be?

RUBY   Fifty cents.

           *He gives her a dollar and while she is
           counting out his change he rallies his powers*

for a final desperate attempt.

MATTHEW Well now, if it isn't too much trouble... I might as well— that is, I'd like to look at... at some sugar.

RUBY White or brown?

MATTHEW Oh, well now ... brown. I'll ... I'll take twenty pounds.

As RUBY is getting the sugar, RACHEL enters. She is surprised to see him.

RACHEL Matthew Cuthbert, what are you doing here?

MATTHEW Ah... brown sugar?

RACHEL Brown sugar!

RUBY Twenty pounds.

RACHEL Twenty pounds! Whatever possessed you to get so much? Marilla never uses it except for porridge or black fruit cake.

MATTHEW I... I thought it might come in handy, sometime. And the rake... I... well now... You see, what I really want to do is...

He leans in and whispers in RACHEL's ear.

RACHEL A dress for Anne?

MATTHEW cringes and nods.

RACHEL Have you something particular in mind?

MATTHEW Na... na...

RACHEL No? Well, Ruby I believe a nice rich brown would just suit Anne, what do you think?

MATTHEW   Na... na... not brown. Something colorful...
ma... maybe with flowers.

RUBY   We have some new Gloria in that's real
pretty. How's this, Mr. Cuthbert?

She shows the fabric. MATTHEW nods.

MATTHEW   It's for the spring, you see, and... and... well,
how many months does it take to make a
pretty dress, anyway?

RACHEL   Why no time at all. I'll make it up for her,
seeing that if Marilla was to make it, Anne
would probably get wind of it before the time
and spoil the surprise.

*MATTHEW makes a feeble attempt at polite
protest.*

RACHEL   No, it isn't a mite of trouble. I like sewing.

MATTHEW   Well now, I'm much obliged and.. .and... I
dunno... but I'd like... I think they make the
sleeves different nowadays to what they used
to be. If it wouldn't be asking too much I— I'd
like them made in the new way.

RACHEL   Puffs? Of course. You needn't worry a speck
more about it, Matthew. I'll make it up in the
very latest fashion.

MATTHEW   Well now... that... would be... Much obliged.

*He hurries out of the store, leaving his brown
sugar.*

RACHEL   I believe that man is waking up after being
asleep for over sixty years.

*RUBY and RACHEL laugh. RACHEL runs
after MATTHEW with the rake.*

RACHEL   Matthew, your rake.

Act Two, Scene Twelve

Green Gables.
ANNE and MARILLA are in the kitchen.
MARILLA is in her best dress and is wearing
her brooch. ANNE is in her best dress too,
severe as ever, and is looking in a hand mirror
while MARILLA brushes her hair.

ANNE   I am so nervous. I mean, Marilla, "class valedictorian". I don't know if I can stand in front of everybody and... speak.

MARILLA   You've been practicing since late April, Anne.

ANNE   Yes, I think I can manage the speech, but there will be singing, Marilla. What if I sing off-key and Gil... some of the boys make fun of me for it or...

MATTHEW enters with a box under his arm.

MATTHEW   He wouldn't dare laugh at the prettiest girl at graduation.

ANNE   Oh Matthew, you are so gallant to say so, but that's impossible. After all, with my red hair and freckles and... Josie Pye has had a dress made for her of pink damask that is so beautiful, I feel sure we will all be lost in her radiance.

MATTHEW sheepishly unfolds the dress from its paper swathing and holds it out with a deprecatory glance.

MATTHEW   Well, we'll just see about that.

ANNE   Why... why, Matthew, is that for me? Oh, Matthew!

ANNE holds up the dress.

MARILLA   Well, I hope you'll be satisfied at last, Anne. There's enough material in those sleeves alone to make a waist, I declare there is.

ANNE   It's beautiful, Marilla. I simply cannot breathe another breath until I have tried on this dress.

ANNE rushes upstairs to try on the dress.

MARILLA   So this is what you have been looking so mysterious and grinning about is it? I knew you were up to some foolishness.

MATTHEW   Well, now I guess that there dress is about as far from foolish as an old fool can be.

MARILLA   The puffs have been getting bigger and more ridiculous right along — they're as big as balloons now. Next year anybody who wears them will have to go through a door sideways.

MATTHEW   Well now, I'm not so concerned about that as I am with Anne feeling like a queen. Think of it Marilla, seems like just yesterday I first set eyes on that gangling little wisp of misery and hope sitting there on the railway platform, and now... Our little girl is going to Queen's College to learn to be a teacher and we did that, Marilla. We grew her up — beats growin' potatoes now, doesn't it?

ANNE comes running on in the dress.

ANNE   *(starting to cry)* Oh, Matthew...

MATTHEW   Why... why, Anne, don't you like it? Well now, well now...

ANNE   Like it! Oh, Matthew! Matthew, it's perfectly
            exquisite. Oh, I can never thank you enough.
            Look at these sleeves! I'm so glad that puffed
            sleeves are still fashionable. It did seem to me
            that I'd never get over it if they went out
            before I had a dress with them.

MARILLA   It's pretty enough all right, but I believe
            there's something missing.

MATTHEW   What's missing?

MARILLA   Well, it's nothing but foolishness but I do
            believe if you were to have a beautiful jewel
            pinned to your dress, you might look just like a
            Queen.

            *MARILLA removes her brooch and pins it on
            ANNE.*

MARILLA   There now.

Act Two, Scene Thirteen

Green Gables.
JOSIE, RUBY and DIANA stand around the
piano singing My Love Is Like A Red, Red
Rose. *RACHEL directs them, joining in when*
she can no longer resist it. MARILLA sits
knitting and enjoying the music. As the song
goes on, MATTHEW enters the parlour and
sits down in an armchair with a long sigh. He
has the paper and eases back in the chair, but
just sits listening. Then the older ANNE
enters and joins in the singing.

THE GIRLS   My love is like a red red rose
              that's newly sprung in June
              My love is like a melody
              that's sweetly played in tune
              As fair art thou, my bonnie lass,
              so deep in love am I
              And I will love thee still my dear,
              'til all the seas gang dry
              'til all the seas gang dry, my dear
              'til all the seas gang dry
              And I will love thee still my dear,
              'til all the seas gang dry

              MARILLA begins to cry. ANNE stops.

ANNE   Marilla, our song has made you cry. Now, I
              call that a positive triumph.

MARILLA   Fiddlesticks. I wasn't crying over some silly
              song. It's nothing but my foolishness. I was
              looking at you and thinking that the little girl
              who came to stay has vanished somehow and
              here is this tall, serious-eyed lady in her
              place.

ANNE   Marilla! I'm not a bit changed, not really. I'm
                only just pruned down and branched out.

MARILLA   Maybe, but I just couldn't help thinking of the
                little girl you used to be, Anne. And I was
                wishing you could have stayed a little girl,
                even with all your queer ways. You've grown
                up now and you're going away and... and I just
                got lonesome thinking it all over.

ANNE   It won't make a bit of difference where I go, I
                shall always be your little Anne who will love
                you and Matthew and dear Green Gables more
                and better every day of her life.

                *ANNE lays her cheek against MARILLA's
                and reaches out a hand to pat MATTHEW's
                shoulder.*

MATTHEW   Well now, I guess she ain't been much spoiled,
                is she, Marilla.

MARILLA   No, I guess you putting your oar in occasionally
                never did much harm after all.

MATTHEW   I reckon that's true.

                He sighs and lies back in his chair.

ANNE   You've been working too hard today, haven't
                you, Matthew? Why won't you take things
                easier?

MATTHEW   Well now, I can't seem to.

MARILLA   You're still driving yourself like a boy of
                twenty.

MATTHEW   Well, I've always worked pretty hard.

MARILLA   Yes, and you'll kill yourself with it yet.

MATTHEW   Well now, I guess I'd rather drop in harness.

RACHEL	Matthew Cuthbert.
ANNE	If I had been the boy you sent for, I'd be able to help you so much now and spare you in a hundred ways. I could find it in my heart to wish I had been, just for that.
MATTHEW	I'd rather have you than a dozen boys, Anne. Just mind you that. I guess it wasn't a boy that took the Avery scholarship, was it? It was a girl — my girl — my girl that I'm proud of. Now you girls sing some more. Even if it's just that one again.
THE GIRLS	'Til all the seas gang dry my dear And the rocks melt with the sun And I will love thee ever more 'Til the sands of life are run.

As they sing MATTHEW opens the paper and reads for a moment, then gasps and stands up, his face strangely drawn and gray. He drops the paper and staggers towards the door. The music fails.

MARILLA	Matthew — Matthew — what is the matter?

MARILLA picks up the paper.

MARILLA	The Abbey Bank has failed. Matthew...

He staggers off.

ANNE	Matthew...

Offstage we hear a crash and a thud.

ANNE	Marilla!

MARILLA rushes off after MATTHEW, followed by RACHEL.

MARILLA	(off, an anguished cry) Matthew!

> *Hearing MARILLA's cry, ANNE rushes towards her, but is stopped by RACHEL who emerges looking very sad.*

ANNE   What's the matter?

RACHEL   You can't do anything for him, Anne.

ANNE   Mrs. Lynde, Matthew isn't...

RACHEL   Yes, child, I've seen it so many times and... Matthew is gone.

> *Scene shift. Girls and MARILLA exit softly singing* Red Red Rose.

Act Two, Scene Fourteen

The Graveyard.
ANNE kneels beside MATTHEW's grave
planting a rose cutting. MARILLA stands
watching.

MARILLA   He always liked those roses the best. Mother brought them out from Scotland. They were so small and sweet on their thorny stems.

ANNE   It makes me feel glad to plant them here by his grave. I miss him so much — all the time — and yet, the world and life still seem very beautiful to me.

MARILLA   Yes.

ANNE   And today Diana said something funny and I found myself laughing. I thought when he died, I could never laugh again. I oughtn't to... it doesn't seem right.

MARILLA   Matthew always liked to hear you laugh.

ANNE   Oh, Marilla, I've had this horrible dull ache ever since he died, but... I can't cry. I can laugh, but I can't cry for him and he loved me so much.

MARILLA begins to sob uncontrollably.
ANNE rushes to her. They hold each other,
both crying.

MARILLA   There — there — don't cry so, dearie. It can't bring him back.

ANNE   Oh, Marilla. The tears don't hurt me like the ache does.

MARILLA   It— it — isn't right to cry so. And I wouldn't do it, but... He's always been such a good, kind brother to me. *(trying to pull away)* God knows best.

ANNE   *(holding her tight)* Oh, Marilla, what will we do without him?

MARILLA   We've got each other, Anne. I don't know what I'd do if you --if you'd never come. It's never been easy for me to say things out of my heart, but... I know I've been harsh with you but... you mustn't think I didn't love you as well as Matthew did. I love you as dear as if you were my own flesh and blood.

    They hug and cry. Then MARILLA draws away.

ANNE   Oh, Marilla. Are you very tired?

MARILLA   Yes, no — I don't know. Dr. Stanley made me see the oculist a few days ago. He says that if I give up reading and sewing entirely and any kind of work that strains the eyes and wear the glasses he's given me, he thinks my eyes may not get any worse and my headaches will be cured. But if I don't, he says I'll certainly be stone blind in six months.

ANNE   Blind!

MARILLA   Anne, think of it.

ANNE   No, Marilla, he has given you hope.

MARILLA   Hope! What am I to live for if I can't read or sew or do anything like that? I might as well be blind — or dead.

ANNE   Marilla!

MARILLA   It's no good talking about it. I must sell Green Gables.

ANNE	Sell Green Gables?
MARILLA	If my eyes were strong I could stay here and look after things and manage, with a good hired man. But now things would only get worse and worse all the time, 'til nobody would want to buy it.
ANNE	You can't sell Green Gables. It's your home.
MARILLA	Use your head, girl. Every cent of our money went in that bank. It won't bring much as it's small and the buildings are old, but it'll be enough for me to live on. Rachel says I can board with her.
ANNE	No!
MARILLA	Oh, Anne, I can't stay here alone.
ANNE	You won't have to stay here alone, I'm not going to university.
MARILLA	Not going to university!
ANNE	I could never leave you alone in your trouble, after all you've done for me.
MARILLA	But Anne, all of your plans....
ANNE	I will make new plans. Mrs. Lynde told me last night they hadn't found anyone for the White Sands school. I'll apply. It won't be as nice or convenient as if I had the Avonlea school, but I can board home and drive myself over to White Sands and back.
MARILLA	Not in winter, child — the wind blows so fierce and the storms...
ANNE	Even in winter I can come home Fridays. We'll be real cozy together, and I'm heart glad over the very thought of staying at dear Green Gables. Nobody could love it as you and I do —

so we must keep it.

They hug again. Musical Bridge.

Act Two, Scene Fifteen

In Front of RACHEL's.
JOSIE is walking by when RUBY and
DIANA come hurrying on.

RUBY

Josie, Josie, have you heard the news? It's all over town. Anne has given up her scholarship and applied for the school at White Sands!

JOSIE

What?

DIANA

She did it so she could take care of Marilla.

RUBY

White Sands, isn't that romantic?

> *RACHEL comes out of her place, having overheard the conversation.*

RACHEL

White Sands, fiddlesticks. Anne's going to teach right here in Avonlea.

JOSIE

What?

RACHEL

The trustees want to offer her the school.

JOSIE

But... but I thought it was promised to Gilbert!

RACHEL

It was, but as soon as I told Gilbert Anne had applied at White Sands, he withdrew his application. He said Anne must have Avonlea and he would go to White Sands.

RUBY

Oh, Gilbert!

DIANA

That is so kind and thoughtful of him, isn't it, Josie?

JOSIE

Yes, it's wonderful.

         JOSIE exits, passing GILBERT.

GILBERT   Hello, Josie....

JOSIE   Oh Gilbert, how could you!

         ANNE enters from the other direction and walks purposefully towards GILBERT.

DIANA   There's Anne.

RUBY   Does she know?

RACHEL   Why of course. I told Marilla as soon as I found out.

ANNE   Mr. Blythe? I—

GILBERT   Anne, I was on my way to see you. I wanted to tell you that I've decided to take the position at White Sands.

ANNE   I... I know. Mrs. Lynde came by, fresh from the trustees' meeting and bursting with gossip.

         GILBERT laughs.

GILBERT   There will never be a secret in Avonlea as long as Rachel Lynde trods the planet.

         ANNE pauses. She sees RUBY, RACHEL and DIANA all watching them. DIANA elbows RUBY. They look at RACHEL.

RACHEL   Well ladies, can I offer you a drop of cordial?

         They go into her house, but RACHEL lingers on until ANNE gives her a very pointed look. She then beams and goes inside.

ANNE   Gilbert, I want to thank you for giving up the school for me. It was very good of you... but you can't...

GILBERT   You can't prevent me.

ANNE   But, I don't think I ought to let you make such
            a sacrifice for... for me

GILBERT   I've already signed papers with the White
            Sands trustees. So, it wouldn't do me any good
            now if you were to refuse Avonlea. So this once,
            at least, I win. *(he laughs)*

ANNE   *(laughs too)* Oh Gilbert, how can I thank you
            for giving up the school for me? It was very
            good of you... and I appreciate it.

            ANNE shakes his hand and he holds on to it.

GILBERT   But, I do have something to ask in return.

ANNE   What?

GILBERT   Forgive me my old fault.

ANNE   I forgave you that day you saved me, although
            I didn't know it. I've been — I may as well
            make a complete confession — I've been sorry
            ever since.

GILBERT   Are we going to be friends after this then?

ANNE   I'm not sure if I could get used to the idea. We
            haven't been good friends but we've been very
            good enemies.

            He laughs and lets go of her hand.

ANNE   Gilbert, do you think we can change something,
            anything for the better?

GILBERT   I know we can.

ANNE   It's just that... my future seemed to stretch out
            before me like a straight road. Now there is a
            bend in it. I don't know what lies around the
            bend.

GILBERT   The best, for both of us... and I believe we can help each other. We're going to be good teachers, Anne, and good teachers are worth their weight in gold.

ANNE   Gilbert, you're a kindred spirit!

GILBERT   "Would that I was, my Lady Elaine."

ANNE   I think we are going to be the best of friends.

ANNE takes his hand and smiles.

ANNE   God's in his heaven, all's right with the world.

The End.